*E*PISCOPACY

EPISCOPACY

Lutheran–United Methodist Dialogue II

Edited by

Jack M. Tuell and Roger W. Fjeld

Augsburg ■ Minneapolis

EPISCOPACY
Lutheran–United Methodist Dialogue II

This book is the report of the Lutheran–United Methodist Dialogue, Series II (1986–1988) held under the auspices of the United Methodist Church, the Evangelical Lutheran Church in America, and the Lutheran Church—Missouri Synod.

Scripture quotations unless otherwise noted are from the New Revised Standard Version Bible, copyright © 1989, by the Division of Christian Education of the National Council of Churches.

Cover design: Judy Swanson

Library of Congress Cataloging-in-Publication Data

Episcopacy : Lutheran–United Methodist dialogue II / [edited by] Jack
M. Tuell and Roger W. Fjeld.
        p.   cm.
    "This book is the report of the Lutheran–United Methodist dialogue, series II
(1986–1988) held under the auspices of the United Methodist Church, the Evangelical Lutheran Church in America, and the Lutheran Church—Missouri Synod"—T.p. verso.
    Includes the common statement from the first series of dialogues, 1977–1979:
A Lutheran–United Methodist statement on baptism.
    Includes bibliographical references.
    ISBN 0-8066-2516-3 (alk. paper)
    1. Episcopacy.   2. Episcopacy and Christian union.   3. Lutheran Church—
Bishops.   4. Methodist Church—Bishops.   5. United Methodist Church (U.S.)
6. Evangelical Lutheran Church in America.   7. Lutheran Church—Missouri
Synod.   8. Methodist Church—Doctrines.   9. Lutheran Church—Doctrines.   I.
Tuell, Jack M., 1923–   .   II. Fjeld, Roger W., 1933–   .   III. United Methodist
Church (U.S.)   IV. Evangelical Lutheran Church in America.   V. Lutheran
Church—Missouri Synod.   VI. Lutheran–United Methodist statement on baptism.   1990.
BV670.2.E53   1990
262′.12—dc20   90-26143
                                                                                CIP

The paper used in this publication meets the minimum requirements of American National Standard for Information Sciences—Permanence of Paper for Printed Library Materials, ANSI Z329.48-1984.   ∞™

Manufactured in the U.S.A.   AF 9-2516

95   94   93   92   91   1   2   3   4   5   6   7   8   9   10

Contents

5

Contents

Preface

It is with great joy that we share with you the following statement "Episcopacy: A Lutheran–United Methodist Common Statement to the Church." It is the fruit of three years of bilateral dialogue involving the United Methodist Church and the churches who were partners in the Lutheran Council in the USA.

Fourteen individuals from the Lutheran and United Methodist churches gathered in six extended conversations seeking to address the topic of episcopacy and, in the process, to make our churches and histories better known to each other. We chose this topic because, as the introduction to the statement notes, "The nature of episcopacy has become a focus of ecumenical discussion and difficulty." Both of our denominations are engaged in discussions that make it imperative that we articulate our views of episcopacy and seek to discover whether we have a common understanding.

The dialogue participants have reached a substantial and unanimous consensus about episcopacy and its relation to the broader topic of ministry in our churches. We have different histories, church structures, and use quite different language to order our ministries. However, we discovered that our basic understandings of ministry and episcopacy are remarkably similar. Through this common statement we report those basic understandings to our churches.

We commend this book as a document worthy of study and dialogue at every level within and between our churches. It invites local gatherings of clergy and lay people, regional gatherings of clergy and bishops, and specialized gatherings of committees and commissions charged with giving leadership in ecumenical matters. The material is intended as a means of beginning those conversations, not ending them. It will have served its main purpose if Lutherans and United Methodists around the world think together about these matters. Genuine Christian unity can emerge through such conversations, more than through the gathering of a small group of appointed dialogue members.

As you read these findings some of you will be disappointed that there are no formal recommendations for fellowship; others of you will be relieved that such recommendations have not yet been put forward. Both attitudes illustrate the reality of our situation as churches. Many among us believe a basis for formal fellowship between United Methodists and Lutherans has already been established. Others believe that there are remaining dialogical tasks and topics before that matter can be given formal consideration. Our respective churches must identify the remaining topics that need to be explored before the question of fellowship can be addressed fully. Those participating in the recently concluded dialogues believe that the remaining topics can and should be addressed in a third and final round of dialogues between our churches.

In closing, the two of us who cochaired this second round of dialogues express our deep appreciation to the fourteen members of our churches who gave of themselves throughout these three years of dialogues and who, together, developed such a strong consensus about the matter of episcopacy. And all of us in the dialogues express our sincere appreciation to our churches for giving us the privilege of serving as members of this dialogue. It is our prayer that the mission of the church and the unity of the church will be served by what we have done.

BISHOP JACK M. TUELL
DR. ROGER W. FJELD

PART ONE

COMMON STATEMENTS

Episcopacy:
A Lutheran–United Methodist
Common Statement to the Church

PREFACE

The Lutheran Council in the United States of America (LCUSA), an agency composed of five Lutheran bodies in the U.S. (the Association of Evangelical Lutheran Churches, the American Lutheran Church, the Lutheran Church—Missouri Synod, the Latvian Evangelical Lutheran Church in America, and the Lutheran Church in America), and The United Methodist Church (UMC), a worldwide church body, jointly agreed in 1983 to hold a second series of dialogues, this time on the theme of episcopacy.

The first series between Lutherans and United Methodists was held between 1977 and 1979 on the theme of baptism. The common statement and supporting papers were published in a special issue of the *Perkins Journal* (34) (1981) and a separate printing of the common statement in pamphlet form was widely distributed.

This second series on episcopacy brought participants together for six times between 1985 and 1987. During this time, the new Evangelical Lutheran Church in America was forming and therefore the Common Statement was distributed by that body and The United Methodist Church.

This Common Statement was first published and distributed in pamphlet form, parallel with the earlier pamphlet on baptism. Selected papers prepared for the dialogue are now included in this volume and should contribute considerably to the ongoing discussion on episcopacy within the larger ecumenical movement.

INTRODUCTORY NOTES

Theological documents sometimes reveal more in what is omitted than in what is stated. Sometimes critical agreements are reached

11

which the reader merely takes for granted. These notes are intended to help the reader review the agreed statement with an eye to a more careful reading.

The Introduction sets the context of the dialogue, reminding the reader of the continuity with the previous United Methodist–Lutheran round on baptism and the relationship of the topic to the World Council of Churches' convergence text on "Baptism, Eucharist, and Ministry." It declares two primary themes of the discussion: that episcopacy is an *office* of the Church (not of its essence) and that it is the *mission* of the Church that determines the shape of that office.

Responsibility and accountability are explored as part of the meaning of oversight (*episcopé*) in Part I A, but there is acknowledgment of other forms of oversight within the Church as well. Paragraph 20 lifts up some of the differences between the two traditions and affirms together in Par. 21 that episcopacy is not of the *essence* of the Church nor does it hold an inherent hierarchical understanding.

Part I C suggests that both traditions take a position of openness to the ordering of the Church in other forms. While each may believe that their form of oversight is both biblical and functional, neither believes that *episcopé* can only be structured as each has known it.

With regard to the practice of the *episcopé* (Part II), there are some clear differences between the traditions, particularly in the conciliar way in which United Methodists understand the collegiality of oversight. The bishops, in their prophetic witness and as symbols of unity, remind the Church of its own nature, but the Dialogue Team concluded that the unity of the Church is not dependent on the unity of the episcopate.

INTRODUCTION

1. The Lutheran and Methodist churches alike arose as reform movements within a large church body. Both sought a renewal in the life of the Church. Neither movement set out to create an independent body. Nevertheless, each finds expression today in distinct churches bearing the names "Methodist" and "Lutheran."

2. For historical and geographical reasons, Lutheran and Methodist churches have had little contact with each other. Our history has been characterized neither by mutual condemnation nor by mutual recognition and fellowship. Over the last twenty years,

however, ecumenical dialogues between Methodists and Lutherans have occurred in a variety of settings. Dialogues sponsored by the Lutheran World Federation and the World Methodist Council culminated in 1984 in the common statement "The Church: Community of Grace." This statement discussed an extensive range of topics and recommended "that our churches take steps to declare and establish full fellowship of Word and Sacrament" (¶ 91). Such fellowship was proposed between the (Lutheran) Church of Sweden and the Methodist Church of Sweden in 1985 and established between the United Evangelical–Lutheran Church of Germany and the Evangelical–Methodist Church in the Federal Republic of Germany and West Berlin in 1987.

3. A series of dialogues between The United Methodist Church and the member churches of the Lutheran Council in the USA was held between 1977 and 1979 on the subject of baptism. "A Lutheran–United Methodist Statement on Baptism" was produced.[1] The experience and results of this dialogue have been an encouragement to the present series of conversations between representatives of The United Methodist Church and of the member churches of the Lutheran Council in the USA on the subject of episcopacy.

4. The nature of episcopacy has become a focus of ecumenical discussion and difficulty. What is the nature of the ministry of oversight exercised by bishops? In what way does this ministry relate to other ministries in the Church? How does this ministry relate to the unity and continuity of the Church? United Methodists and Lutherans approach these questions from similar situations. United Methodists and the majority of American Lutherans have clergy called bishops, who play prominent leadership roles.[2] As the following common statement makes clear, our traditions have understood the ministry of the bishop as a form of the office of ministry shared by all clergy and have not understood the episcopal office to be of the essence of the church. Methodists and Lutherans face similar difficulties in our relations with churches which place a different emphasis on the office of bishop. This series of dialogues began with the hope both of furthering Lutheran–Methodist understanding and of contributing to the wider ecumenical discussion of the ministry of oversight.

5. In the New Testament, the term "bishop" does not appear to have a single distinct meaning. At places, it appears to be interchangeable with presbyter (e.g., Acts 20:17, 28). By the end of the second century, however, "bishop" had come to refer to a head of the church in a particular place. The nature of the office has

varied greatly over the history of the Church. Nevertheless, basic ecclesiastical structures (e.g., congregations and dioceses) were headed by bishops. This pattern remained that of almost all of Christianity before and after the Reformation.

6. In recent years, new attempts have been made to understand the nature of the office of bishop. Typical of these attempts is the understanding of episcopal ministry in *Baptism, Eucharist and Ministry, The COCU Consensus,* and a variety of bilateral dialogues.[3]

7. Lutheran and Methodist understandings of episcopacy are colored by our respective histories. Both movements encountered resistance from bishops in their initial attempts to carry out their mission. Both Methodists and Lutherans finally faced a situation in which the only choice they could see was between remaining obedient to episcopal leadership and remaining true to their mission in the gospel. In each case, the latter option was chosen. Our relation to episcopal leadership has been an ecumenical difficulty for both of our churches ever since. Within our own churches, however, episcopal leadership, under a variety of titles, has been respected and valued. Out of our histories and theological reflection we offer this common statement in the continuing endeavor to clarify our own mind and practice, to deepen understanding between our traditions, and to further discussion in the wider Church that seeks to serve the God who makes all one.

Part I. Ecclesiology, Ministry, and Episcopacy

A. Episcopé, Mission, and the Nature of the Church

8. Lutherans and United Methodists each understand themselves to belong to the one Church:

> a congregation of [the] faithful . . . in which the pure Word of God is preached and the Sacraments duly administered according to Christ's ordinance.[4]

> the assembly of all believers among whom the Gospel is preached in its purity and the holy sacraments are administered according to the Gospel.[5]

The life of the one Church is inseparable from the presence within it of the Spirit who moves it to mission. Stated succinctly, this mission is to be a witness to the gospel of the justifying, sanctifying, and liberating Reign of God which has come and still comes to us and to the world in Jesus Christ. In this mission, the unity, holiness, catholicity, and apostolicity of the Church are realized.

9. This mission is carried out in a variety of ministries, empowered by the diverse gifts of the Spirit. Through these ministries, the Spirit not only points to God's activity in Christ, but also effects the redeeming and reconciling presence of Jesus Christ and the Reign of God inseparable from Jesus Christ.

10. The most important standard by which all ministries within the Church are to be judged is the mission which they seek to further. This standard is to be applied both to the general nature and structure of a ministry and its concrete execution. All aspects of ministry are to be judged by the question: do they further the fundamental mission of the Spirit within the Church?

11. The constant application of this criterion is part of the necessary oversight (*episcopé*) of ministry that must occur within the Church. This oversight is carried out first of all and principally through the divinely ordained pastoral office but then also in many ways by various persons and groups of persons from the local congregation to the most inclusive international structures. We trust that through faithful oversight of ministry by the entire Church the Spirit is at work, preserving the Church in mission.

12. While responsibility for oversight must finally rest with the entire Church, some persons, conferences, assemblies, boards, etc., are given responsibility for specific tasks of oversight. Oversight is thus itself a form of ministry within the Church. That specific responsibilities of oversight are given to some, however, does not take from the wider community responsibility and authority to oversee those who carry out specific ministries of oversight. Those who carry out ministries of oversight remain accountable to the community of believers. Such "oversight of oversight" is one way the mutual accountability of all ministries within the Church is realized. Ultimate accountability, of course, is always to the Word of God.

13. Our churches and all churches throughout the world must ask whether present forms of oversight are adequate to mission in the present and the future. While being mindful of the importance of continuity and the wisdom of our forebears, we must be open to different forms of oversight, whether new or old, that will better aid present and future mission.

B. Episcopacy and the Nature of Ministry

14. Every member of the Church is called to ministry through baptism. Ministry is an activity of the entire Church and of each individual within it.

15. While all Christians share the ministry of the Word, we acknowledge God's gift of an ordained ministry, the public pastoral office. United Methodists and Lutherans typically refer to this ministry with different terms (a ministry of Word, Sacrament, and Order or a ministry of Word and Sacrament). Although this difference in language points to differences in how we understand ordained ministry, we have come to see that our different terms refer to the same ministry. Lutherans and United Methodists alike affirm this ministry as necessary to the church. The ordained minister presides in the proclamation of the Word, the celebration of the sacraments, and the administration of churchly order.[6]

16. Every church must find ways in which oversight of ordained ministry can be exercised. This oversight is concerned with all aspects of ordained ministry: its administrative organization, its faithfulness to the mission of Christ, the pastoral care it gives and receives.

17. In our churches a primary means of oversight is the office of bishop. We find this means of providing for oversight theologically and practically desirable. We do not, however, understand this oversight to be the exclusive prerogative of the bishop. Oversight is to be carried out in cooperation with other persons within the church. In addition, we do not see the episcopal office as the only acceptable means by which oversight of ordained ministry can be realized. Ecumenical relations with churches which carry out oversight through, e.g., a presbytery pose no special problems in themselves for Lutherans or United Methodists. The episcopal office is not of the essence of the Church.

18. Bishops are themselves ordained ministers. United Methodists and Lutherans understand the distinctive ministry of the bishop to be a form of the single ordained ministry. We have thus emphasized the unity of the ministry of bishops with the ministry of all the ordained. Our churches rightly grant authority to bishops to carry out their necessary ministry. Some activities within our churches are typically performed only by bishops. Nevertheless, the authority of the bishop derives from the office and its responsibilities; it never inheres in the person of the bishop in distinction from the office. That certain activities are typically carried out only

by bishops derives from the relation between the activity reserved to the bishop and the ministry of the bishop. We do not understand bishops in their persons and distinct from their office to possess capacities and powers not possessed by all Christians.

19. As is true for all authority within the Church, any authority exercised by a bishop is subordinate to the authority of the Bible, which for Lutherans and United Methodists is the"primary source and guideline for doctrine."[7]

20. The bishop's ministry of oversight appropriately extends to the oversight of ordination itself. United Methodist bishops preside at ordinations by themselves ordaining the candidates. Lutheran bishops conventionally attest the call of the congregation and authorize the service of ordination. With different frequency in our different churches, they participate in the ordination. None of our churches requires that a person ordained in another church by someone other than a bishop undergo a Lutheran or United Methodist ordination before entering the ordained ministry within our churches. United Methodists and Lutherans thus do not understand episcopal ordination to be of the essence of ordained ministry.

21. Our churches and the Church throughout the world must understand and organize episcopal and other ministries in ways that affirm their diversity and mutual accountability. An understanding in which other ministries become intrinsically subordinate to, under the control of, or derived from the ministry of the bishop is to be rejected.

C. Episcopacy and the Universal Church

22. Lutherans and United Methodists today face similar ecumenical proposals concerning episcopacy (e.g., *Baptism, Eucharist and Ministry,* the *COCU* proposals, *Facing Unity*).[8] We face these proposals with similar understandings and practices of episcopacy. Our churches are also engaged in parallel studies of the nature of ministry and episcopacy.

23. Neither United Methodists nor Lutherans understand their ordering or structuring of ministry to be the only theologically acceptable one. Thus, we are open to the possibility of restructuring our ministries, including episcopacy, for the sake of more effective mission.

24. Any proposal for a reordering of episcopacy in our churches must a) indicate how such a reordering will serve the mission

entrusted to our churches, b) in no way imply that the ordained ministry carried out by our churches has lacked anything essential, and c) not imply that the proposed reordering is of the essence of the Church. Additional criteria may be needed for judging proposals for a reordered episcopacy.

25. While Lutherans and United Methodists alike celebrate the achievements represented by the ecumenical proposals of recent years, whether these proposals meet the criteria specified in ¶ 24 is disputed within our churches.[9]

26. The detailed and critical discussion in our churches of these ecumenical proposals is a necessary step in the formation of an understanding and practice that will open us to the unity Jesus Christ desires for the Church. Further refinements of the proposals presently under discussion and the development of new proposals must continue.

PART II. PRACTICE OF EPISCOPE´ IN THE TWO TRADITIONS

A. Historic Practice

27. Lutherans and United Methodists developed our present structures of oversight through a combination of theological reflection and historical circumstance. Both traditions initially moved away from an episcopacy in historical succession with reluctance.[10]

28. United Methodists and Lutherans have learned from our differing histories that a ministry of oversight like that of bishops is a practical necessity. Such a ministry is needed for the empowering and equipping of the entire body of the saints for mission. In recent years, the structure and practice of our ministries of oversight have become more similar. Many Lutherans have given greater recognition and authority to synodical and district ministries of oversight, while United Methodists have sought to strengthen the accountability of the episcopacy to other ministries.[11]

29. Both Lutherans and United Methodists have sought organizational structures that will both be efficient and embody ecclesiological principles to which we are committed. United Methodists and Lutherans in the United States have sought to preserve the accountability of bishops to the rest of the church, e.g., by protecting against individual abuses of power that obscure mission. We have found such structures of accountability important to our life. We offer the ways we elect and review bishops and interrelate

episcopal and other ministries as a contribution to the ecumenical discussion.

30. Lutherans have not shared the United Methodist experience with bishops who are "itinerant, general superintendents," yet assigned to specific areas. United Methodists view each bishop as a bishop of the whole church and the Council of Bishops as an expression of the collegiality of oversight. The United Methodist practice of episcopacy raises issues about the universal responsibility of each bishop and of the college of bishops that need to be reflected on by all churches. Discussions about a reordering of the ministry of oversight should examine the particular experience of Lutherans and United Methodists.

31. Lutherans and United Methodists have in recent years appropriated new language and concepts in our thought about and practice of the ministry of oversight. We together recognize ourselves to be in a process of continual reform in our ministry of oversight and hope for structures that will more effectively aid the mission that unites us.

32. The United Methodist Church and the churches forming the Evangelical Lutheran Church in America call women and men to the ordained ministry. On the basis of Scripture, theological principle, and experience, these churches strongly affirm their commitment to the presence of women and men in all forms of ordained ministry, including the office of bishop. The Lutheran Church—Missouri Synod, on the basis of Scripture and theological principle, does not ordain women to the pastoral office.

B. The Ministry of the Bishop

33. Since the ministry of bishops is a form of the ministry shared by all ordained ministers, the common pastoral, liturgical, and proclamatory tasks of the ordained ministry should be central to the ministry of bishops. Our churches need to find ways in which the preaching of the Word and the celebration of the sacraments can be given greater priority within the total activity of our bishops.

34. We agree that the entire ministry of bishops has a pastoral character. However, our churches are organized in ways that hinder the development of pastoral relations between bishops and the clergy and laity.

35. As persons called to oversee and exercise the ordained ministry, bishops in their total ministry should serve the unity, holiness, catholicity, and apostolicity of the church.

36. In their preaching and teaching, bishops serve the apostolicity and catholicity of the Church. In our churches, bishops have recently spoken out on issues of concern to the Church and the world. We have profited from their voice. Whether their ministry of oversight gives bishops a special voice in the decisions of the church is a question for both Lutherans and United Methodists.

37. As their ministry of oversight focuses on the pure preaching and teaching of the gospel, bishops serve the unity of the Church. United Methodists have in the past understood their bishops as an important symbol of the unity of the Church. Lutherans have understood that the unity of the Church is created by the Word of God, manifested in the preaching of the gospel and the administration of the sacraments. Lutherans are not of one mind on the ecumenical role of bishops, as recent studies indicate. Neither Lutherans nor United Methodists equate the visible unity of the Church with the unity of the episcopate. Nevertheless, we are open to discussion of the special ecumenical role that may be played by bishops and the episcopacy.

38. In the witness to the gospel of the grace of God which they share with all Christians and all pastors, bishops serve the holiness Christ shares with the Church. The visibility of bishops to the Church and the world gives their witness particular prominence within the Church's total witness. The words and lives of those who lead the church can have a profound effect. Our churches need to seek leaders who will reflect Christ in their total life and ministry.

CONCLUSION

39. The Church looks to Jesus Christ as the Shepherd and Bishop of our souls (I Pt 2:25). United Methodists and Lutherans reflect on episcopacy with this fundamental conviction in mind. We bring to this reflection practices of episcopacy that have much in common. Although we have each struggled with questions of authority and freedom, we have recognized the importance of a ministry of oversight as one ministry among others in the Body of Christ. Leadership from our bishops and presidents has often aided greater unity and effectiveness. Nevertheless, we have together insisted that no particular structure of oversight is of the essence of the Church. Church-dividing difficulties have developed because of this insistence. We offer our common convictions in the hope

that this obstacle can be overcome as all churches reconsider how they can serve the single and unifying mission of Christ.

Notes

1. The statement was signed by all representatives, except those from the Lutheran Church—Missouri Synod (LC–MS).
2. A synodical or district president within the LC–MS carries out a ministry of oversight similar to that of bishops in the other participating churches. The term "bishop" is used throughout this statement to refer to LC–MS presidents. In Lutheran and Methodist churches in other parts of the world, other titles are also used for those who exercise episcopal leadership (e.g., praeses, superintendent, ephorus).
3. For example, *The Report of the Lutheran–Episcopal Dialogue Second Series 1976–1980* (Cincinnati: Forward Movement Press, 1981); James E. Andrews and Joseph A. Burgess, eds., *An Invitation to Action: A Study of Ministry, Sacraments, and Recognition*, The Lutheran–Reformed Dialogue Series III, 1981–1983 (Philadelphia: Fortress Press, 1984).
4. Article 13, The Articles of Religion of the Methodist Church. In *The Book of Discipline*, Part II, Section 2, ¶ 68. Cp. The Confession of Faith of the Evangelical United Brethren Church, Article 5.
5. Augsburg Confession, Article VII. In *The Book of Concord: The Confessions of the Evangelical Lutheran Church*, trans. and ed. by Theodore G. Tappert, et al. (Philadelphia: Fortress Press, 1959), p. 32.
6. Cp. Lutheran–Methodist Joint Commission, *The Church: Community of Grace* (Geneva: Lutheran World Federation; Lake Junaluska: World Methodist Council, 1984), ¶ 37. A typically greater Methodist stress on the administration of churchly order is reflected in Methodist language of a ministry of Word, Sacrament, and Order. Lutheran ministers of Word and Sacrament are also called upon, however, to administer churchly order.
7. "Our Theological Task," in *The Book of Discipline*, Part II, Section 3, ¶ 69, p. 78. Cp. Formula of Concord, Epitome, Rule and Norm, 1.
8. See *Baptism, Eucharist and Ministry*, Faith and Order Paper III (Geneva: World Council of Churches, 1982); *Covenanting Toward Unity: From Consensus to Communion. A Proposal to the Churches from the Consultation on Church Union* (Baltimore: Consultation on Church Union, 1985); *The COCU Consensus: In Quest of a Church of Christ Uniting*, ed. Gerald F. Moede (Baltimore: Consultation on Church Union, 1985); Roman Catholic/Lutheran Joint Commission, *Facing Unity: Models, Forms and Phases of Catholic–Lutheran Church Fellowship* (Geneva: Lutheran World Federation, 1985). Typical of the understanding of episcopal ministry in these proposals is ¶29 of the third section of *Baptism Eucharist, and Ministry:*

   Bishops preach the Word, preside at the sacraments, and administer discipline in such a way as to be representative pastoral ministers of oversight, continuity and unity in the Church. They have pastoral oversight of the area to which they are called. They serve the apostolicity and unity of the church's teaching, worship, and sacramental life. They have responsibility for leadership in the Church's mission. They relate the Christian community in their area to the wider Church, and the universal Church to their community. They, in communion with the presbyters and deacons and the whole community, are responsible for the orderly transfer of ministerial authority in the Church. (¶ M29)

9. Four of the participating churches have responded officially to BEM. The responses can be found in *Churches Respond to BEM: Official Responses to the "Baptism, Eucharist and Ministry"* text, 3 vols., Faith and Order Papers 129, 132, 135, ed. Max Thurian (Geneva: World Council of Churches, 1986–87), Vol. 1, pp. 28–38. Vol. 2, pp. 79–84, 177–199, Vol. 3, pp. 131–141.

10. Attitudes toward episcopacy were mixed among early Lutherans and early Methodists. While statements about the desire to retain episcopacy in historical succession can be found in the Lutheran Confessions (e.g., Apo. 14), their interpretation is a matter of dispute.

11. For this history, see James K. Mathews, *Set Apart to Serve: The Meaning and Role of Episcopacy in the Wesleyan Tradition* (Nashville: Abingdon Press, 1985), and Ivar Asheim and Victor R. Gold, *Episcopacy in the Lutheran Church? Studies in the Development and Definition of the Office of Church Leadership* (Philadelphia: Fortress Press, 1970). The Asheim and Gold volume does not cover important recent developments in American Lutheranism.

PARTICIPANTS VOTING YES

Lutherans

Dr. Roger W. Fjeld (ALC)
Chairperson of the Delegation
President, Wartburg Theological
   Seminary
Dubuque, Iowa

Dr. George Bornemann (LCMS)
Oveida, Florida

Dr. Raymond M. Bost (LCA)
Newberry, South Carolina

Dr. Eugene F. Klug (LCMS)
Chairman, Dept. of Systematic
   Theology
Concordia Theological Seminary
Ft. Wayne, Indiana

Dr. Todd Nichol (ALC)
Professor of Church History
Luther Northwestern Theological
   Seminary
St. Paul, Minnesota

The Rev. Kenneth T. Ponds
   (AELC)
Chaplain, Starr Commonwealth
   Schools
Albion, Michigan

Dr. Michael J. Root (LCA)
Professor of Ethics & Systematics
Lutheran Theological Southern
   Seminary
Columbia, South Carolina

United Methodists

Bishop Jack M. Tuell
Chairperson of the Delegation
California Pacific Conference of
The United Methodist Church
Pasadena, California

Dr. Jerome Del Pino
Pastor in Charge, Wesley UMC
Springfield, Massachusetts

Dr. Diedra Kreiwald
Professor of Christian Education
Wesley Theological Seminary
Washington, D.C.

Dr. Arthur J. Landwehr
Senior Pastor, First UMC
Evanston, Illinois

Dr. Gerald F. Moede
General Secretary, Consultation on
Church Union
Princeton, New Jersey

Ms. Carolyn Oehler
Director, Northern Illinois
Conference Council on
Ministries
Chicago, Illinois

The Rev. Janice Riggle Huie
Copastor, Manchaca UMC
Manchaca, Texas

Bishop Roy I. Sano
Denver Area Conference of The
United Methodist Church
Denver, Colorado

NONVOTING

Staff
Dr. Joseph A. Burgess, Exec. Dir.
Division of Theological Studies
Lutheran Council in the USA*
New York, New York

Observer
Dr. John F. Johnson
DTS Standing Committee Rep.
Concordia Theological Seminary
St. Louis, Missouri

Staff
Dr. Jeanne Audrey Powers
Associate General Secretary
General Commission on Christian
Unity and Interreligious
Concerns
The United Methodist Church
New York, New York

*The Lutheran Council in the USA went out of existence on January 1, 1988 with the formation of the Evangelical Lutheran Church in America. Administrative staff responsibilities for future ELCA-UMC bilateral relations now rest with the ELCA Office for Ecumenical Affairs, Chicago, Illinois.

A Lutheran–United Methodist Statement on Baptism

INTRODUCTION

As participants in the Lutheran–United Methodist bilateral consultation, which has met six times since 1977 and has now concluded its work, we report with gratitude to our churches the pastoral, liturgical, and evangelical concord and concern that we have discovered in our discussions.

It is fundamental to this report to note that our Lutheran and United Methodist churches acknowledge Scripture as the source and the norm of Christian faith and life, and share with the whole catholic church in that Christology and that trinitarian faith which was set forth in the ecumenical Apostles' and Nicene Creeds. We also share the biblical Reformation doctrine of justification by grace through faith. We are agreed that we are justified by the grace of God for Christ's sake through faith alone and not by works demanded of us by God's law. We also recognize the common emphasis on sanctification as a divinely promised consequence of justification. We affirm that God acts to use the sacraments as means of grace. As heirs of the Reformation, we share a heritage of scriptural preaching and biblical scholarship. We also share a hymnic tradition, care for theological education, and concern for evangelical outreach.

We have continually recognized the validity of the acts of baptism administered in accord with Scripture in our churches. While this recognition testifies to our considerable agreement in doctrine and practice, it rests finally upon the shared acknowledgement of baptism as an effective sign of God's grace. First and foremost, baptism is God's gift, act, and promise of faithfulness. The entire life of faith and even our attempts to articulate a common understanding of God's prior act of grace are but a response of praise and thanksgiving.

The acknowledgement of God's gift as validly bestowed in the acts of baptism administered in United Methodist and Lutheran churches entails the recognition of the shared benefit of the work of the Holy Spirit among us. Thus we are called to confess the scandal of whatever disunity or party spirit may still exist among us and between us, lest we be found to despise God's gift. Our unity in Christ and in one Spirit is the unity of those who have been washed and forgiven, incorporated into Christ's death and resurrection, and called together for witness and service in his world until he comes again. This unity made manifest in baptism is an inauguration and foretaste of the rule of God in all of life.

Thus we are offering to our churches the following affirmations, implications, and recommendations as tangible expressions of our hope that our churches and congregations will seek further means for achieving a fuller manifestation of our God-given unity in Christ, of our sharing in one Spirit and one baptism.

AFFIRMATIONS

1. We accept as valid all acts of baptism in the name of the Trinity using water according to Christ's command and promise (Matt. 28:18–20).

2. We affirm that baptism is the sacrament of entrance into the holy catholic church, not simply a rite of entrance into a particular denomination. Baptism is therefore a sacrament which proclaims the profound unity of the church (I Cor. 12:13; Gal. 3:27–28). Baptism is a gift of God for the upbuilding of the Christian community.

3. We affirm that grateful obedience to the divine invitation obliges all believers to be baptized and to share the responsibility for baptizing.

4. We affirm that baptism is intended for all persons, including infants. No person should be excluded from baptism for reasons of age or mental capacity.

5. We affirm with Scripture that God gives the Holy Spirit in baptism:

  ■ to unite us with Jesus Christ in his death, burial, and resurrection (Rom. 6:1–11; Col. 2:12);

25

- to effect new birth, new creation, newness of life (John 3:5; Titus 3:5);
- to offer, give and assure us of the forgiveness of sins in both cleansing and lifegiving aspects (Acts 2:38);
- to enable our continual repentance and daily reception of forgiveness and our growing in grace;
- to create unity and equality in Christ (I Cor. 12:13; Gal. 3:27–28);
- to make us participants in the new age initiated by the saving act of God in Jesus Christ (John 3:5);
- to place us into the Body of Christ where the benefits of the Holy Spirit are shared within a visible community of faith (Acts 2:38; I Cor. 12:13).

6. We affirm that in claiming us in baptism, God enables Christians to rely upon this gift, promise, and assurance throughout all of life. Such faithful reliance is necessary and sufficient for the reception of the benefits of baptism.

7. We affirm that baptism is both the prior gift of God's grace and the believer's commitment of faith. Baptism looks toward a growth into the measure of the stature of the fullness of Christ (Eph. 4:13). By this growth, baptized believers should manifest to the world the new race of a redeemed humanity, which puts an end to all human estrangement based upon distinctions such as race, sex, age, class, nationality, and disabling conditions. In faith and obedience, the baptized live for the sake of Christ, of his church, and of the world which he loves. Baptism is a way in which the church witnesses to the faith and proclaims to the world the Lordship of Jesus Christ.

Implications and Recommendations

1. Baptism is related to a Christian community and (except in unusual circumstances) should be administered by an ordained minister in the service of public worship of the congregation.

We agree that baptism should not be a private act. In communities where United Methodist and Lutheran congregations exist, they can support one another as they resist pressure for private family baptisms. Normally, for reasons of good order, the ordained officiate at baptisms, but any person may administer the sacrament in unusual circumstances.

2. Lutherans and United Methodists agree that prebaptismal instruction of candidates and their parents (or surrogate parents) is of crucial importance.

Therefore, we encourage ministers and congregations to take this instruction seriously and to support one another as they resist pressure to minimize such instruction.

3. The Christian community has the responsibility to receive and nurture the baptized. When infants or children are baptized we regard it as essential that at least one parent, surrogate parent, or other responsible adult make an act of Christian commitment to nurture them in the Christian faith and life.

There may be circumstances in which the refusal of baptism is appropriate because this condition has not been met. Both United Methodist and Lutheran pastors can support one another by respecting and interpreting the action of one of them who has refused to administer baptism.

Sponsors (or godparents) may support the parent, surrogate parent, or other responsible adult in this act of commitment but are not substitutes for such a committed individual.

4. When a Christian family is partly Lutheran and partly United Methodist, the nurture of the baptized child is of primary concern. Here an opportunity also exists to display Christian unity in the midst of diversity.

It is important for one congregation to assume primary responsibility to nurture the child in the Christian life.

Where one parent is more active than the other, it is recommended that the sponsoring congregation be the congregation of the more active parent.

It is recommended that the pre-baptismal instruction be given by the pastor of the sponsoring congregation; or joint instruction under both pastors can take place, as this will enrich both traditions.

5. We believe baptism is not repeatable.

Because we understand baptism as entrance into the church, we do not condone rebaptism of persons on any grounds, including those related to new Christian experience or change of denominational membership.

Since United Methodists and Lutherans recognize one another's baptism, we violate the integrity of our faith, pervert the meaning of baptism, and impair our relation with other baptized Christians if we rebaptize.

6. When instructed persons have made their profession of faith for themselves in baptism, their Christian initiation requires no separate rite of confirmation.

Baptism is sacramentally complete even though the baptized Christian looks forward to a lifetime of Christian instruction and growth through regular reaffirmations or renewals of the baptismal covenant.

7. We respect each other's practice of confirmation.

We rejoice that both communions have an appreciation for the lifelong need for a pastoral and educational ministry. The baptized should be given frequent opportunity to reflect upon the meaning of their covenant through confirmation, sermons, curricula, and other such means.

While orientation to the history, liturgy, and practice of the denomination and of a particular congregation is appropriate for persons who transfer from one of our denominations to the other, a further confirmation rite should not be required.

8. Baptism witnesses to Christian unity, and therefore it enables transfer between our denominations.

Because we believe that baptism is the fundamental initiation into the church, we affirm our oneness in Jesus Christ as taking precedence over our denominational divisions.

When persons transfer their membership between our denominations, they should not feel that they have thereby broken their earlier baptismal and confirmation promises. Pastors should provide opportunity for those transferring to make public reaffirmation of their baptism with the new congregation and denomination in an appropriate manner.

Each denomination affirms the pastoral and nurturing ministry of the other denomination and gladly commits members to the care of the other denomination when its own denomination does not provide an adequate congregational family for those members.

Because we are baptized not into a denomination or into a particular congregation only but into the one church of Jesus Christ, therefore in communities where both Lutheran and United Methodist congregations exist, efforts may be made to share mutually in baptismal celebrations, thereby showing forth our essential unity.

9. United Methodist and Lutheran theology and practice allow baptism to be administered in various modes, including immersion, pouring, and sprinkling.

We agree that whatever mode is used, baptism is an act in which the use of water is an outward and visible sign of the grace of God. The water of baptism, therefore, should be administered generously so that its sign value will be most effectively perceived by the congregation.

10. *The celebration of baptism should reflect the unity of the church which baptism proclaims.*

Because in baptism the contemporary church is united to the historic church, baptismal rites should draw upon the ancient traditions of the church and also should serve to illustrate the catholicity of the church in our time. We recommend that in addition to the normative trinitarian baptismal formula in accordance with Matthew 28:19, the celebration of baptism include the renunciation, the Apostles' Creed, and the prayer of thanksgiving over the water.

We urge the common development of liturgical formulations for the rite of baptism by the liturgical agencies of our respective churches.

CONCLUSION

This document represents the consensus of the undersigned members of the dialogue team after three years of intense discussion and prayerful deliberation. We commend it to our churches for their study and action. We hope it will serve as an impetus and resource for dialogue among Lutheran and United Methodists in local communities and throughout our churches.

Washington, D. C.
December 11, 1979

PARTICIPANTS VOTING YES

Lutherans

Dr. J. Thomas Tredway (LCA)
Chairperson of the Delegation
President
Augustana College
Rock Island, Illinois

Bishop Darold H. Beekman (ALC)
Southwestern Minnesota District
Willmar, Minnesota

Dr. Harry Huxhold (AELC)
Pastor
Our Redeemer Lutheran Church
Indianapolis, Indiana

The Rev. Margaret Krych (LCA)
Assistant Professor
Lutheran Theological Seminary at
  Philadelphia
Philadelphia, Pennsylvania

Dr. Klaus Penzel (LCA)
Professor of Church History
Perkins School of Theology
Southern Methodist University
Dallas, Texas

Dr. Alice Schimpf (ALC)
Professor of Religion
Capital University
Columbus, Ohio

Dr. David L. Tiede (ALC)
Associate Professor of New
Testament
Luther Northwestern Seminaries
St. Paul, Minnesota

Dr. Joseph Burgess
Staff
Executive Director
Division of Theological Studies
Lutheran Council in the U. S. A.
New York, New York

United Methodists

Bishop Jack M. Tuell
Chairperson of the Delegation
Portland Area
The United Methodist Church
Portland, Oregon

Dr. E. Dale Dunlap
Vice-Chairperson of the Delegation
Dean and Professor of Theology
Saint Paul School of Theology
Methodist
Kansas City, Missouri

The Rev. Hoyt Hickman
Assistant General Secretary for the
Section on Worship
Board of Discipleship
The United Methodist Church
Nashville, Tennessee

Professor Ethel R. Johnson
Methodist Theological School in
Ohio
Columbus, Ohio

Dr. Kenneth Kinghorn
Professor of Church History
Asbury Theological Seminary
Wilmore, Kentucky

The Rev. Arthur J. Landwehr
Senior Minister
First United Methodist Church of
Evanston
Evanston, Illinois

The Rev. Martha Rowlett
Sierra Madre, California

Dr. Laurence H. Stookey
Professor of Preaching and
Worship
Wesley Theological Seminary
Washington, D. C.

Dr. Thomas Trotter
General Secretary
Board of Higher Education and
Ministry
The United Methodist Church
Nashville, Tennessee

Dr. James F. White
Professor of Christian Worship
Perkins School of Theology
Southern Methodist University
Dallas, Texas

The Rev. Jeanne Audrey Powers
Staff
Assistant Ecumenical Staff Officer
The United Methodist Church
New York, New York

30

PARTICIPANT VOTING NO

Lutheran

The Rev. Jerrold A. Eickmann
(LCMS)
Assistant Professor of Systematic
Theology
Concordia Seminary
St. Louis, Missouri

PARTICIPANTS ABSTAINING

Lutherans

The Rev. Arthur J. Crosmer
(LCMS)
Vice-Chairperson of the Delegation
Pastor
Immanuel Lutheran Church
Twin Falls, Idaho

Dr. Willis L. Wright (LCMS)
President
Alabama Lutheran College
Selma, Alabama

Lutheran Designations:

AELC—Association of Evangelical
Lutheran Churches
ALC—The American Lutheran
Church
LCA—Lutheran Church in
America
LCMS—The Lutheran Church—
Missouri Synod

BACKGROUND

1

Bishops in the Lutheran Tradition: *The Book of Concord* and Later Lutheranism

Among Lutherans Article IV of the Augsburg Confession is embraced as the *articulus stantis aut cadentis ecclesiae*, the article by which the church stands or falls.[1] As the confessional statement of justification by faith, it is a revolutionary assertion with radical correlates. The first is a new understanding of the ministry. Article V answers the question implicit in Article IV. If justification is by faith, where does faith come from? Faith comes from the Word of God. And "To obtain such faith God instituted the office of the ministry, that is, provided the Gospel and the sacraments. Through these, as through means, he gives the Holy Spirit, who works faith, when and where he pleases, in those who hear the Gospel."[2]

The confessors of these two sentences overturn a massive complex of inherited ideas as well as practices and reshape the doctrine of the ministry. A spoken word requires speaking and therefore speakers. Speaking and speakers make a ministry distinguished not by rank but by assigned activity. Lutherans would say the ministry is a matter of *Amt* rather than *Stand*, of office rather than status. One expects the Confessions to speak of people appointed or a class ordained, but instead one hears of Word and sacraments, of things to do. The emphasis is on activity and function rather than on order. God commands one Word to be spoken in sermon and made visible in sacraments. The church in turn calls on people to tell and show the Word, to fill the office of the ministry. In its simplicity and substance the evangelical doctrine of the ministry is a correlate of the doctrine of justification and a carefully conceived departure from the received tradition.

Given simplicity and substance, it is surprising to find the Augsburg Confession and its Apology complicated and compromising when it comes to bishops. Simplicity and substance can be traced to the thoughts of Luther and Melanchthon. Complexity and compromise intrude when princes, jurists, and theologians gather at Augsburg to prepare the Confession and to negotiate the fate of the evangelical movement.

LUTHER AND MELANCHTHON

It has long been argued that two doctrines of the ministry compete in Luther's thought.[3] Some passages can be interpreted to suggest that the church's public ministry is through the medium of the priesthood shared by all believers. Other texts emphasize the divine institution of the public ministry. A close reading of the texts themselves suggests that the debate has been misconceived.[4] Luther insists on the divine institution of the ministry. Nowhere does he assert that the public ministry emerges by delegation from the Christian congregation. For Luther the dialectic generating the doctrine of the ministry is not defined by poles of ministry and church, but by the event of Word and congregations gathered by the Word. It is God who has spoken and it is God's Word that requires speaking. The ministry is divinely ordained, and the church has nothing of its own to transfer to any of its members. With regard to the ministry, the only questions for the church are "Who shall do the speaking?" and "How shall they be elected, called, installed, and supervised?" It is in answering these questions that Luther will give different answers. He will read the Roman hierarchy lessons in history and theology; in changing contexts he will caution those to his left about the sanctity of the call, and urge congregations caught up in the reforming movement to elect and call pastors of their own choosing. He will also address the issue of episcopacy in these situations.

Luther shaped his notion of the ministry in the early stages of the conflict with Rome. In *The Babylonian Captivity of the Church* he stresses the common priesthood of all Christians and their prerogative of assigning the public duties in the congregation to one of their number by mutual consent.[5] He ceases to regard ordination as a sacrament and commands bishops as well as priests to know and preach the gospel.[6] The same themes are reiterated in *To the Christian Nobility.* Again the divine institution of the ministry is asserted as is the common priesthood of all Christians.[7] The steady refrain of the ministry as office and work rather than status is repeated.[8] Bishops are called to ordain on behalf of the community, and Luther argues that in an emergency situation it would be fitting to ordain without the presence of a bishop.[9] A new theme—and one that will be heard clearly in the Confessions—is introduced when Luther advises bishops to cease interfering in temporal affairs.[10]

The circumstances of a movement without a program eventually forced Luther to think about the shape of the public ministry and episcopacy in evangelical congregations. For the congregation in Leisnig he wrote a tract with the incendiary title *That a Christian Assembly or Congregation Has the Right and Power to Judge All Teaching, and to Call, Appoint, and Dismiss Teachers, Established and Proven by Scripture*. One passage encapsulates his advice to the evangelical congregations:

> Since a Christian congregation neither should nor could exist without God's word, it clearly follows . . . that it nevertheless must have teachers and preachers who administer the word. And since in these last and accursed times the bishops and the false spiritual government neither are nor wish to be teachers—moreover, they want neither to provide nor to tolerate any, and God should not be tempted to send new preachers from heaven—we must act according to Scripture and call and institute from among ourselves those who are found to be qualified and whom God has enlightened with reason and endowed with gifts to do so.[11]

Later in the same year Luther would extend the argument against the bishops in his tract for the Bohemian Utraquists, *Concerning the Ministry*. He assures the Bohemians that the church is among them through the presence of the Word. Since they have been deprived of the ministry of the Word by the oppressive measures of the Roman church, they must elect bishops of their own choosing who will supervise the calling of pastors by the congregations.[12] The evangelical bishops may, if they wish, gather and elect one from among their number to serve as a "rightful and evangelical" archbishop charged with the task of visitation.[13]

By 1525, with his ordination of Georg Rörer, Luther had removed ordination from the number of the sacraments and taken it from the bishops' hands into his own and those of other pastors.[14] In addition he had altered the understanding of ordination by ecclesiastical superiors. Rather than mediate sacramental grace, ordination would serve to confirm the call of the congregation and provide opportunity for intercession among evangelicals. He had ceased to regard a *successio personalis* as necessary to the bishop's office. The new understanding of ministry recognized only one divinely ordained office: the ministry of preaching and sacraments. Divisions of responsibilities among servants of the ministry would be for the sake of jurisdiction. The episcopal office would exist only *jure humano* among evangelicals. For the most part bishops or superintendents would be charged with visitation and other duties of oversight instead of with sacramental functions.

By 1527 visitations were under way in Saxony. The ecclesiastical visitors commissioned to undertake the necessary tasks—lay as well as clerical—were guided by *Instructions* written by Luther's younger colleague, Philip Melanchthon. By this time Melanchthon's approach to the ministry was similar to Luther's. In fact, as early as the *Loci Communes* of 1521, Melanchthon had begun to work with distinctions between human laws and divine ordinances that would lead him in Luther's direction when practical questions of reform were at stake.[15] For example, a clear argument for the origin of church and ministry in the Word of God is evident in a theological opinion on the *jus reformandi* prepared for the elector in 1526.[16] Although sometimes more yielding in negotiations, Melanchthon, like Luther, seemed to have retained a consistent view of both ministry and episcopacy until the end of his life. He steadily asserted that there is one office of the ministry, that the ministry is by and of the Word, and that duties of oversight may be added as an arrangement *jure humano* for the sake of service to the church. In the so-called *Wittenberg Reformation* of 1546 he wrote:

> It is necessary to distinguish from the episcopal polity, bound to place, person, and due succession, offices and human regulations—the ministry of the gospel instituted by God and continually restored by his great mercy which perpetually serves the church and is not bound to certain places, persons, and human laws, but to the gospel.[17]

In 1528 Melanchthon's *Instructions for the Visitors* was published under a preface by Luther. The visitations in Saxony, begun on the elector's orders in 1527, were a radical usurpation by both lay and clerical members of the church of episcopal authority; and the *Instructions* assumes the abrogation of the Roman episcopacy. It is taken for granted that there will be an office of "Superintendent."[18] The duties of the superintendents are to oversee the parishes and benefices of their jurisdictions in order to insure sound doctrine, faithful preaching, and the administration of the sacraments. The superintendents are also charged with a care for godliness among the clergy. Where there is error, the superintendent is charged with correcting it and bringing the obstinate to the attention of the elector. Where there are vacancies, candidates are to be presented to the superintendent for examination. There is no mention of ordination. Ordination may be assumed, or the Saxons may have done without it for a time. Examination and call may have been regarded as sufficient for entry into office.[19]

Luther's preface to the *Instructions* documents his developing attitude toward the episcopacy and introduces a theme that will figure prominently in the Augsburg Confession. Of the bishops' neglect of visitation, he says: "This office has fared like all holy and ancient Christian doctrine and order—it has become the farce and contempt of the devil and Antichrist with awful and terrible destruction of souls."[20] What to do?

> We would like to have seen the true episcopal office and practice of visitation re-established because of the pressing need. However since none of us felt a call or definite command to do this . . . we have respectfully appealed to the illustrious and noble prince and Lord, John, Duke of Saxony . . . that out of Christian love (since he is not obligated to do so as a temporal sovereign), and by God's will for the benefit of the gospel and the welfare of the wretched Christians in his territory, His electoral grace might call and ordain to this office several competent persons.[21]

Luther's care in distinguishing the elector's office of love as believer and neighbor from his duties as a temporal sovereign is consistent with his earlier insistence that temporal lords and bishops untangle their secular and spiritual affairs. Luther argues that while princes are not to be bishops, they are charged with preserving peace and unity of faith. This passage anticipates an important element in the text of Article XXVIII of the Augsburg Confession.[22]

WORMS TO AUGSBURG

In 1521 the Edict of Worms declared Luther and his followers under the ban. Political and military circumstances, however, prevented Emperor Charles from exacting compliance with the Edict and events of the following years strengthened the evangelical position.

At the first Diet of Speyer in 1526, empire and papacy stood confronted by a host of evangelical estates rather than a solitary monk, and more lenient terms were established. It was agreed to hold a general council or a provincial council for Germany as soon as convenient. In the meantime each of the estates was to govern its conduct and hold its faith according to conscience. This reprieve gave the evangelical movement crucial years to put down deep roots in German soil.

When the second Diet of Speyer was summoned for 1529 events took a turn that threatened the evangelicals. The emperor had made peace with the French and the pope and was free to turn his attention to German affairs. At the same time, political scandal had tarnished the cause of the reformation and left its adherents disorganized. The text of the summons to the Diet was an ominous sign. It revoked the terms of the recess of the first Diet of Speyer and called for implementation of the Edict of Worms. In the remonstrance that gave Protestants their name, the evangelical princes at Speyer protested that this was a violation of the promise of a council and that in matters of faith, conscience could not be coerced.

The tenuous situation prompted the Protestant estates to ponder the question of alliance and three preliminary alliances were concluded in the years 1524–1526. The firebrand of the Lutheran princes, Philip of Hesse, hoped for a larger federation and, with the help of Jakob Sturm of Strasbourg, succeeded in organizing a secret federation during a meeting at Speyer in 1529. Luther and others, however, insisted that political alliances required unity in doctrine. This resulted in a series of colloquies and the creation of several confessional statements, including the Schwabach articles upon which the first part of the Augsburg Confession was based. The Marburg colloquy between the Lutherans and the Swiss reformers was an attempt to find a way toward a larger federation, however, the resulting disagreement over the Lord's Supper prevented an alliance. Eventually the alliance at Speyer crumbled, and hopes for Protestant unity foundered on division of theological opinion.

In January 1530 a hopeful sign appeared when Charles V issued a summons for another diet to meet at Augsburg. The tone of the summons was irenic and promising, and the Saxons greeted it with hope.[23] John the Steadfast of Saxony instructed Luther, Melanchthon, John Bugenhagen, and Justus Jonas to deliberate and prepare a statement explaining faith and usage in Saxony. The result was the so-called Torgau articles, which formed the basis of the second part of the Augsburg Confession.

Without allies, but hopeful that reconciliation might be achieved, the Saxon Lutherans developed a policy of compromise to bring to Augsburg. It was conceived by the Saxon princes, the chancellor Gregory Brück, and Melanchthon; it had hesitating support from Luther and Jonas. The strategy was to seek legal recognition of the evangelical reform in exchange for the reintroduction of a stringently reformed episcopacy where it had been abolished. The research of Wilhelm Maurer has recently emphasized the importance of the Torgau articles in this context and put scholars in a position to trace the evolution of the strategy of compromise in the various drafts of those articles.[24]

The Torgau articles became the nucleus of the compromise the Saxons took to the Diet. The proposal was to accept a strictly limited jurisdiction for bishops in return for the elimination of the oath requiring renunciation of evangelical doctrine, toleration of communion in both kinds, reform of the mass, and priestly marriage. It was not a platform likely to commend itself to Philip of Hesse or the stridently anti-episcopal representatives of the Lutheran cities. For the Saxons, however, it offered the possibility of reconciliation with the emperor and had the added advantage of distancing them from the more radical positions taken by the Anabaptists.[25]

CONFESSION

On the way to the Diet Melanchthon and the Saxon party began work on the statement to be presented at Augsburg. An early draft of a preface, written by Melanchthon in April 1530, documents three aspects of the Saxon policy.[26] First, the Saxons had taken the summons to Augsburg as a hopeful sign and looked to Charles for an impartial and perhaps favorable hearing. Second, they planned to stand alone at the Diet and to only apologize for their own reforms. Third, their statement was initially intended to explain and defend reforms already undertaken in Saxony. As such it was to be brief and concise.

The appearance of John Eck's *404 Articles* caused a change of strategy. Eck's calumny prompted the Lutherans to consider collaborating in preparing a longer and more complete statement of their faith. The brief apology originally contemplated by the Saxons was to become a full confession of faith made in common with other Lutheran estates. A first draft was finished by May 11 and sent to Luther who, under the ban and unable to attend the Diet, was staying at Coburg in order to be as near to the proceedings as safely possible.

An early draft of Article XXVIII may have been included in the version of the Confession sent to Luther on May 11.[27] This article, titled "of the Power of the Keys," continues the line of argumentation established in the third Torgau articles. It dismisses the contention that the pope alone possesses the power of the keys along with the argument that by the power of the keys the pope has the authority to appoint and remove kings—that the keys give the pope supreme temporal authority. As distinct to the medieval tradition, the power of the keys is redefined as "the command to preach the Gospel, and to reprove and forgive sinners in the name and on behalf of Christ. Thus the power of the keys is now only spiritual government. . . ."[28] It is conceded that the pope may bear temporal responsibilities, but these are added by a "human donation which we do not accept."[29] It is further argued that the pope has no power to institute usages contrary to the gospel or to bind consciences to observing these usages. A reference to Acts 5:29 is introduced, to become a refrain of the confessional argument. "If now these laws and dispensations are contrary to God's Word, we are in duty bound to obey God rather than man. . . ."[30] Finally, the functional equivalence of all ministerial ranks is asserted.[31]

A second recension of Article XXVIII appears in the oldest extant form of the complete Confession.[32] This draft, titled "Of the Power of the Church," omits mentioning the pope and is evidence of a renewed attempt to accommodate episcopal jurisdiction in some form of compromise. Again the point of departure is the distinction of temporal and spiritual authority. The power of the sword or civil authority is distinguished from the spiritual sword or the power of the Word of God to forgive sins. "Since the power of the Church grants eternal things and is exercised only by the ministry of the Word, it does not interfere with civil government, no more than singing or arithmetic interferes with civil government."[33] It is conceded that bishops may assume civil responsibility and own property, but in these capacities they hold a different and distinct office than that of bishop. "When therefore a question arises concerning the jurisdiction of bishops, civil authority must be distinguished from ecclesiastical jurisdiction."[34] The bishops are prohibited from introducing usages contrary to the gospel and binding consciences to them. When the test case of the transfer of the

Sabbath to Sunday by ecclesiastical convention is advanced, the statement argues that this was permissible for the sake of order, but that the observance of Sunday could not be considered in the category of things meriting grace or making satisfaction for sin.[35] The conclusion of the second draft is explicit:

> It is not our design to wrest the government from the bishops, but we ask that they allow the Gospel to be purely taught and that they relax some few observances which cannot be kept without sin. But if they make no concession, it is for them to see how they shall give account to God, for having by their obstinacy, caused a schism.[36]

A third draft of Article XXVIII resembles the confessional statement in its final form as it was read on June 25 and printed in the *Editio Princeps*. In addition to refinements in argumentation and documentation, it shows an increasing awareness of the need to defend the emerging evangelical church order. The terms of the compromise are somewhat tightened by the addition of this statement on the power of the civil authorities: "Where the ordinaries fail, princes are bound, if willingly or against their will, to dispense justice to their subjects, for the maintenance of peace to avoid discord and serious unrest in the land."[37] The statement recalls the opening passage of Luther's *To the Christian Nobility* and comments in the preface to the *Instructions for the Visitors*. Its intent is to curtail the jurisdiction of the bishops in two senses. It instructs the princes to step in and maintain order in places where bishops fail in their duties as temporal sovereigns. And, recalling Luther's mention of the Emperor Constantine, it implies that in cases of grave religious disorders the princes have the right and even the duty to intervene and secure religious harmony in the interests of civil peace.[38]

NEGOTIATION

Even before the Confession was read in its final form on June 25, Melanchthon had begun secret negotiations with imperial secretaries Cornelius Schepper and Alfonso Valdes. Apparently with the knowledge and consent of the Lutheran princes, he had proposed that negotiations between the contending parties be confined to abuses and specifically to four points: marriage of the clergy, communion in two kinds, reform of the mass, and church property. He was prepared to concede episcopal jurisdiction. For three days prior to the reading of the Confession, it appeared that these negotiations might succeed, but on July 20 they were abruptly terminated by action of the Protestant princes.

Following the presentation of the Confession and the reading of the papal Confutation, Melanchthon and Brück made persistent efforts to keep the possibility of reconciliation alive and to sustain the offer of a compromise on episcopal jurisdiction. Both Saxons were prepared to be generous in the matter of bishops. For example, Melanchthon wrote to Joachim Camerarius on July 19, "I have embraced those things which are of first importance. I concede total jurisdiction and whatever is fitting to the bishops."[39] As the negotiations proceeded, evangelical support for the compromise dwindled. Philip of Hesse led the defections. By the end of the proceedings at Augsburg all the evangelical states signing the Augsburg Confession except electoral Saxony had disavowed the offer to reintroduce episcopacy. For them the confessional compromise was a dead letter, and the episcopate had been repudiated in the most polemical terms. The reply of the *Curia* only sealed the fate of the compromise.

Luther could not have been surprised by the denouement. Restless in his confinement at Coburg, he bombarded his friends at Augsburg with a series of letters urging courage and warning against compromise. He feared that Melanchthon would concede too much in a moment in which Christ would be confessed before the world. He knew, however, of the compromise on episcopacy and gave it reluctant support.

How reluctant his support is obvious from his *Exhortation to All Clergy Assembled at Augsburg* published in early June. The *Exhortation* is an account of the progress of the reforming movement from his days alone at Worms to the moment in which a host of confessors stood prepared to give account of their faith before the emperor. After an extended discussion of faith and practice, Luther devotes attention to the case of the bishops who, he says, have kept an ignoble silence in response to the summons of the reformers, but present themselves as perspicacious enough to see a new gnat in the sun.[40] If the cause of the gospel was left up to bishops such as these, the church would perish.[41] The true bishop's office has of necessity devolved on the pastors and preachers of the evangelical movement.[42] Nevertheless, Luther is prepared to endorse the confessional compromise on episcopacy under four conditions. First, they must surrender the office of preaching to evangelical preachers. Second, no gold is to change hands; the preachers will work without remuneration. Third, the bishops may retain their temporal dignities and responsibilities "for the sake of peace." Fourth, episcopal jurisdiction may be restored only if the bishops agree to allow the gospel to be preached in complete freedom. In summary, Luther concedes that it may be too late.

> The offer is this: we will perform the duties of your office; we will support ourselves without cost to you; we will help you remain as you are; and we will counsel that you have authority and are to see to it that things go right. What more can we do? . . . See to it that you do not break our backs in two and try our patience too far. If you are going to suppress the upright heretics who are carrying you along, take care what becomes of you. Unfortunately the game is no longer in our hands, as it was before, for the devil has taken it away from us. We can assuredly help you no longer.[43]

There is a mordant thrust to Luther's humor in the *Exhortation*, intimating that he knows his terms are so stringent that they will not be accepted and that his hopes for a division of responsibilities are unrealistic. "Someone at this point might think it silly to hear that the endowment bishops should rule the churches, since it is well known that they cannot and will not learn how. . . ."[44] Luther's answer revealed precisely what he was willing to concede under the notion of a reformed episcopal jurisdiction: the right of patronage or of confirming call. "I know well, sad to say, that it is true. But in order that the wicked people may see that we seek peace and that nothing is lacking in us, I can put up with their providing parishes and pulpits with clergymen and thus help to administer the gospel."[45] That he would compromise no further is plain from his characteristic statement, "The Lutherans remain masters because Christ is with them and they remain with him. . . ."[46]

Luther's suspicions were confirmed as the negotiations continued. He wrote to Augsburg urging that no further concessions be made and at one point advocated making a political settlement without further attempts at reaching a common confession. Even this more realistic hope was not realized by the time that negotiations came to an end in September.

THE ARGUMENT

Article XXVIII is embedded in the Augsburg Confession as the offer of a compromise never achieved. It is, however, a closely written rationale for an episcopacy acceptable to Lutherans. The argument may be summarized under eight points.[47]

(1) The spiritual and temporal swords are to be distinguished (pars. 1–4). If bishops wield temporal power they do so not as bishops and by divine right but as officers of state and by human right (pars. 16, 18–19).

(2) The power of bishops is the power of the keys. The power of the keys is the power to preach the gospel, to forgive and bind sins, and to administer the sacraments. This is a spiritual office effective only through the Word of God. Temporal power proceeds from physical compulsion and is not to be confused with the power of the keys (pars. 5–17).

(3) The power of the bishops to preach, forgive sins, judge doctrine, and excommunicate is the power of the Word alone. This is not to be accomplished by physical force. Obedience is due the bishops only when their prescriptions do not conflict with the Word of God (pars. 20–22). If bishops have jurisdiction in other matters it is by human right. If they are negligent in these or other duties the princes are obligated to step in and take action (par. 29).

(4) Bishops and other pastors (*episcopi seu pastores*) exercise equivalent authority not only in the power of the keys but also in jurisdictional questions (pars. 30, 53).

(5) If the bishops institute practices contrary to the gospel they are to be disobeyed (pars. 23–28).

(6) Bishops are permitted to regulate the church for the sake of order, love, and peace and for this reason obedience is due them (pars. 53–54).

(7) The bishops have no authority to institute anything contrary to Scripture or to promulgate requirements that make grace or justification conditional upon their fulfillment (pars. 30–52, 56–58).

(8) If the bishops will dispense with usages that cannot be kept without sin, if they will permit communion in both kinds, if they will allow clergy to marry, and if they will abandon the oath requiring renunciation of evangelical doctrine, they may retain their dignity and the obedience of believers. If not, believers should disobey them and the bishops should beware of offering occasion for schism (pars. 69–78).

The Apology of the Augsburg Confession refines, but does not advance the argument of the Confession. By referring to the distinction between the *potestas ordinis* and *potestas jurisdictionis*, it does however clarify the duties and prerogatives of the bishop.[48] The *potestas ordinis* or "power of order" is the ministry of Word and Sacraments. The *potestas jurisdictionis* or "power of jurisdiction" is the power to excommunicate and absolve the excommunicated (although not to apply temporal punishments). It is again emphasized that the bishop's power to regulate the church is only for the sake of order and peace, and that the bishop may not institute any practices contrary to the gospel.[49] The powers of order and jurisdiction are not equivalent to the power of tyranny.[50] The Roman Catholic opposition had attempted to circumvent these arguments by citing the statement of Heb. 13:17, "Obey your leaders. . . ." Melanchthon's response to this may be taken as the epitome of the confessional position on the authority of bishops: "This statement requires obedience to the Gospel; it does not create an authority for the bishops apart from the Gospel."[51]

Although he was entangled in ecclesiastical and imperial politics, Melanchthon managed to make a coherent and subtle case based on a double application of the notion of the two kingdoms. The argument turns around the question of the proper place of the prince bishops in church and empire. Article XXVIII of the Confession argues that where prince bishops retain civil duties and rights they do so by political convention; as such they are subject to the limitations outlined, for example, in Luther's *On Temporal Authority: To What Extent It Should Be Obeyed*.[52] Civil obedience is due these prelates in their capacities as princes and not as shepherds of Christ's flock. If they wield the temporal sword, it is as princes and not as bishops. As princes they are subject to God's rules for human politics, the unwritten statutes of the kingdom on the left. Yet because the two kingdoms are intermingled, they also—still in their capacities as princes—have obligations to the kingdom on the right. As princes they are also believers and prohibited from establishing laws or exacting compliance with laws that tempt other believers to disobey God or transgress against the gospel. If they attempt to do so, they are to be met with disobedience. On the other hand, if they maintain a godly and just rule, they are to be obeyed as princes.

As pastors, the bishops are servants of the kingdom on the right. As Christian ministers their obligation is to wield the keys through preaching and the sacraments. Obedience is due only to the Word that the bishops preach. "If they teach, introduce, or institute anything contrary to the Gospel, we have God's command not to be obedient in such cases. . . ."[53] The implicit and crucial point is that the only acceptable bishops will be evangelical pastors who acknowledge that their jurisdiction over their provinces is *jure humano*, for the sake of order and edification. The only divinely given task of the bishop is identical to that of the parish pastor: to preach the Word and administer the sacraments. "What ever other power and jurisdiction bishops may have in various matters . . . they have these by virtue of human right."[54] Yet as princes are subject to the rules of two kingdoms, so also are bishops. The church is a human as well as divine congregation. "We are not dreaming about some Platonic republic . . . ," as Melanchthon put it in his defense of Articles VII and VIII in the Apology.[55] As a human community, the church like the state lives in both the kingdom on the right and the kingdom on the left—thus the willingness of the Confession and Apology to allow bishops to regulate the church for the sake of order, love, and peace. The bishops have the left-handed task of ordering and administering the church while taking care to remember their dual citizenship. As in their capacities as princes, bishops as overseers of the church cannot legislate or rule in contravention of the First Commandment or the gospel.

The remaining Lutheran symbols continue to defend the position taken by the Augsburg Confession and its Apology. In the Smalcald Articles Luther concedes that true bishops might ordain, but as civil rulers they only condemn and persecute pastors.[56] Evangelicals should follow the ancient tradition of the church and ordain without the bishops.[57] In the Treatise on the Power and Primacy of the Pope, Melanchthon emphasizes the functional equivalence of "pastors, presbyters, or bishops" [*vocentur pastores, sive presbyteri, sive episcopi*], and argues again that distinction of rank in the ministry is by human authority and not divine institution.[58] He also reemphasizes that ordination is given as a gift to the church as a whole and when regular (that is, Roman Catholic) bishops become enemies of the gospel and do not acknowledge evangelical doctrine, the churches retain the right to ordain pastors of their own choosing.[59] The Treatise concludes with a harsh condemnation of the Roman Catholic bishops, charging that they defend impiety, support the cruelty of the pope, usurp jurisdiction not properly theirs, observe unjust laws, and defraud the church.[60] *The Formula of Concord's* silence on the matter of episcopacy—especially in the case of Article X on "Church Usages" where it might have been raised in connection with questions of things *adiaphora* or of magisterial authority—indicates that for evangelicals the matter had been closed within fifty years of the presentation of the Augsburg Confession.

BISHOPS IN EARLY LUTHERANISM

The history of early Lutheranism reflects a widespread acceptance of the confessional position.[61]

In Germany an office of "Visitor" or "Superintendent" became the reformatory model. Occupants of this office were often assisted by consistories who took care of certain matters, including the difficult questions of marriage laws cited in the Confessions. The superintendents were appointed *jure humano* to look after the needs of the church: to preach, to teach, to visit in the congregations, to oversee their growth, to look to their health, to adjudicate disputes, and to ordain. There were a few experiments with an episcopacy on the medieval model but none endured.

The situation was similar in Scandinavia. As a part of the coup that brought him to power in 1536, Christian III of Denmark deposed the Roman Catholic bishops of Denmark. On September 2, 1537, John Bugenhagen of Wittenberg, a pastor with a priest's ordination, ordained seven new bishops for the Reformed Church of Denmark, thus breaking the *successio personalis* of the medieval Danish episcopate. In Norway two bishops were allowed to continue after the introduction of the Reformation. One of the bishops, Geble Pedersson of Bergen, was an *electus;* he had been elected but never consecrated. The other, Hans Reff of Oslo, was deposed for a time but then allowed to return to his see; he was not consecrated again.

Events in Sweden and Finland followed a more complicated course. When Gustavus Vasa assumed the Swedish throne in 1523, five sees stood vacant. He sought to fill these in approved canonical fashion and succeeded in the case of Petrus Magni, who was consecrated with papal approval in Rome in 1524. In 1528 Petrus Magni consecrated three bishops, and in 1531 Laurentius Petri was consecrated archbishop (possibly by Petrus Magni). Petri performed a final consecration in 1536. Continuity of the inherited order was breached when the king called on two Germans, Conrad von Pyhy and George Norman, to reorganize the Swedish church on the continental model. After their arrival, superintendents were appointed by the king and installed by other ecclesiastics. During this transitional period it seems that the consecrations of Michael Agricola and Paulus Juusten for sees in Finland by Botvid Sunesson of Strängnäs were regarded as valid episcopal consecrations. Some continuity was restored in Sweden with the appointment of Laurentius Petri Gotha as archbishop in 1575. Among the participants in the consecration was Juusten. Scholarly opinion is divided over whether an episcopal *successio personalis* survived in the Swedish church during this period.[62] But it is certain that the prevailing Lutheran pattern eventually established itself in Sweden. For the most part the term "bishop" was discarded, superintendents were charged with duties of oversight, and pastors as well as bishops conducted ordinations. That these things are not reflected in the present episcopal regime in the Church of Sweden is the result of developments in the nineteenth century.[63]

Throughout Scandinavia the episcopal office was dramatically reformed. The office of oversight was regarded as an ecclesiastical convention rather than a divine invention. In the generations following the reform, the Scandinavians generally called their ordinaries "superintendent" (superintendent or superattendant) rather than "bishop." They did not return to the older usage for generations. Although forms of cooperation with the civil authorities differed in the various states, duties of oversight in the Scandinavian churches were prescribed much as in Germany. An example of the new model prelate in both Scandinavia and Germany was Peder Palladius of Denmark. A glance at his *Visitation Book* shows how he was unlike his medieval predecessors and the degree to which he realized the ideals of Luther, Melanchthon, and the Lutheran confessors. In light of this conformity to the ideals of the first reformers, it is not surprising that the Lutheran interpretation of the office of bishop exercised widespread influence among other Protestants. For example, it is known that the Danish model of the office of oversight provided patterns for the polity of the Church of Scotland.[64]

WHAT A BISHOP IS NOT

In spite of this early ecumenical influence, it is difficult to see how the Lutheran Confessions can inform contemporary ecumenical conversation on questions of *episkopé* and episcopacy. It is tempting to say, as someone recently has, that the Lutheran Confessions tell us what a bishop is not.[65] Of course it is true that there are no prince bishops, and we are not disturbed by many of the problems that troubled the confessors. The context has changed so much that some of what is here does not serve us.

But I think the Confessions and the early Lutheran tradition offer us more than a little help in shaping our life together. To start with the Confessions anticipate the consensus of contemporary exegetes that no form of church order or polity is prescribed as normal in the New Testament. In this respect they leave Lutherans with nothing to talk themselves out of. Instead the Confessions insist on locating the origin of the church in the Word of God and in finding the task of the ministry in that Word. They leave the church to its freedom for the rest. Lutherans have yet to realize the possibilities inherent in this radical approach to ministry. Finally, the Confessions offer some realistic advice about the life of the church—in the world for which it was created and in the two kingdoms in which it inescapably lives. On the one hand, the Confessions acknowledge the need for order and oversight in the congregations and larger manifestations of the church. On the other hand, the confessors insist that the Word of God cannot be muffled or mutilated in the name of order or oversight. If circumstances have changed in more than four hundred years since the Confessions were written, the church's situation has not. It appears Lutherans (not least in the context of ecumenical dialogue) still have things to learn from the Lutheran Confessions. Perhaps partners in ecumenical conversation can best help Lutherans step into the possibilities they offer. Lutherans and Methodists in dialogue may prove that to be the case.

2

Bishops in the Methodist Tradition: Historical Perspectives

*This essay is dedicated to J. Warren Jacobs:
disciple of Jesus Christ, ecumenist,
scholar, humorist, and friend.*

WESLEY'S EPISCOPACY

The Mission Context

In accounting for the rise and expansion of Methodism, (and of its ministry and episcopacy), mission needs to be seen as a primary paradigm. To be faithful to the *missio dei* was John Wesley's primary motivation; it accounted for most of what he said and did. In his mind ministry, as part of a larger whole, had to do with mission as well. This point could be illustrated in different ways.

For example, people needed to hear the gospel from a preacher, they needed to be called to believe, to "flee from the wrath to come," to live lives of "scriptural holiness." The physical needs of poverty-stricken people needed to be cared for—classes, dispensaries, small work projects, modest schools, loan funds, etc. People also needed to worship regularly around the Lord's Table for he called them to attend their local parish church and partake of the Lord's Supper regularly.

> Whatever facilitated mission seemed right to him. "I would inquire," he wrote on June 25, 1746, "what is the end of all ecclesiastical order? Is it not to bring souls from the power of Satan to God, and to build them up in His fear and love? Order, then, is so far valuable as it answers these ends, and if it answers them not, it is nothing worth."[1]

This basic point need not be argued. To both John and Charles Wesley, faithful mission demanded wholeness and unity. Thus in England, John Wesley believed it was his responsibility to fulfill that part of the mission of the church which had been neglected, to reconstitute the apostolic obedience of the church. So he and his preachers rode throughout Britain preaching that the Holy Spirit might awaken faith in their hearers, that the church might hear a whole gospel. But in accordance with his concern for the oneness of the church, which was also constitutive in its mission, Wesley did not allow unordained preachers to administer the sacraments in his societies; he felt that the administration of the sacraments was being legitimately cared for by the ordained priests of the Church of England. "Itinerant Methodist preachers had a vocation which, by every canonical criterion, demanded the presupposition of a faithful active ministry both pastoral and sacramental in the contiguous living church."[2]

As Colin Williams puts it:

> Wesley struggled to an amazing degree to keep unity within the Church, because he believed that not only the true preaching of the Word, but also the unity and continuity of the Church were vital to her mission.[3]

The Role of John Wesley in Early Methodism

At first Wesley expressed the belief that his ministry was like that of the scriptural *episkopos,* overseeing or supervising the whole movement. This was his place for more than forty years, until after his eightieth birthday.

For many years John Wesley struggled to maintain the unity of his movement with the national church by steadfastly refusing to ordain his preachers, even after he became convinced that in the early church the presbyter/bishop were of the same order and that he had a theological right to proceed. He could abide by this position as long as the mission of the church as he understood it was not being damaged. In England he could appoint preachers to preach a more authentic gospel (he scrutinized, educated, and tested them very carefully), and his people could receive the sacraments in the Church of England. His movement was one of reform and completeness.

But from 1784 on, when there was no more Church of England in the United States, his scruples were ended. The mission of the church was being adversely affected, and thus not only could he ordain, he must.

Almost forty years earlier he articulated the insight upon which he then acted:

Lord King's *Account of the Primitive Church* convinced me many years ago that bishops and presbyters are the same order, and consequently have the same right to ordain. . . . I was determined as little as possible to violate the established order of the National Church to which I belonged.

But the case is widely different between England and North America. Here there are bishops who have a legal jurisdiction: in America there are none, neither any parish ministers. So that for some hundreds of miles together there is none either to baptize or to administer the Lord's Supper. Here, therefore, my scruples are at an end. . . .[4]

There was, however, an incongruity in Wesley's thinking. He believed that to exercise a preaching ministry all one needed was the call of God, whereas to exercise a priestly ministry the full approval and juridical apparatus, including ordination, was necessary. Thus he could send unordained preachers over the entire country with good conscience while insisting that his people continue to receive weekly Eucharist at the parish church where ordained priests ministered.

For many years the Methodist movement in the new world was initiated and continued by lay people. Even the preachers Wesley sent from England were not ordained. When the war broke out in 1776, most of the priests of the Church of England (who had provided Methodists with sacramental ministry) and most of the Methodist preachers returned to Britain. By 1784 there were about fifteen thousand Methodists who had no access to Baptism or the Lord's Supper.

When the war ended, Wesley took action. In the Minutes of 1786 he described the situation:

Judging this to be a case of real necessity, I took a step which, for peace and quietness I had refrained from taking many years; I exercised that power which I am fully persuaded the great Shepherd and Bishop of the Church has given me. I appointed three of our laborers to go and help them, by not only preaching the word of God, but likewise administering the Lord's Supper, and baptizing their children throughout that vast tract of land.[5]

So that his American followers would understand his intention in ordaining Thomas Coke as a superintendent (already a priest in the Church of England), Wesley drew up and sent his famous "Circular Letter," dated September 10, 1784. He wrote:

I have appointed Dr. Coke and Mr. Francis Asbury to be joint Superintendents over our brethren in North America; as also Richard Whatcoat and Thomas Vasey to act as elders among them, by baptizing and administering the Lord's Supper . . .

5. If any one will point out to me a more rational and scriptural way of feeding and guiding those poor sheep in the wilderness, I will gladly embrace it.

6. They are now at full liberty simply to follow the Scriptures and the Primitive Church. And we judge it best that they should stand fast in that liberty wherewith God has so strangely made them free.

John Wesley[6]

Wesley's Thought on Ordination and Episcopacy

Historians have understood the evolution in John Wesley's mind on the subject of ministry. In January 1746 a reading of King's *An Inquiry into the Constitution, Discipline, Unity, and Worship of the Primitive Church* convinced Wesley that bishops and presbyters had been, and still were, of the same order, different only in grade.[7]

From this new insight he deduced that there might be a variety of church governments. He still believed that there were three orders of ministry although the New Testament prescribed none.

In a letter of July 3, 1756, Wesley wrote:

I still believe the episcopal form of church government to be scriptural and apostolical. I mean, well agreeing with the practice and writing of the apostles. But that it is prescribed in Scripture, I do not believe. This opinion, which I once zealously espoused, I have been heartily ashamed of, ever since I read Bishop Stillingfleet's "Irenicum."[8]

In 1784, explaining his ordination of Coke, Whatcoat, and Vasey, he based his right, not on the theory that anyone could ordain, or that ordination was only a sociological phenomenon, but rather that he had ordained as a presbyter/bishop, and that ordination by presbyters had been done validly (more often than he knew) in church history.

What is clear is that Wesley did not equate succession with a juridical chain of laying on of hands by persons called bishops. To him, apostolicity was vital, and orderly transmission of a commission was apparently equally essential. There are other indications that suggest how seriously Wesley regarded the bishop's role in ordination.

Application for Ordination. First there is an intriguing story of Wesley applying for ordination for John Jones, one of his preachers from a wandering Orthodox bishop named Erasmus. This story illustrates how seriously he took orderly transmission and the sign of ordination as late as 1783.[9]

Second, there is good evidence that Wesley's setting apart Coke as a superintendent was intended to be an ordination, not merely an installation. Although the ordination was irregular, he used the word "ordination" to describe his action in his diary. Even though John did not use the word "ordain" in public documents, Charles Wesley understood that John intended his laying on of hands to be ordination. The hymn Charles wrote upon hearing the news of Coke's ordination did not get into the *Hymn Book*, but illustrates his realization that John meant to ordain:

> So easily are Bishops made
> By man's or woman's whim?
> Wesley his hands on Coke hath laid,
> But who laid hands on him?

> Hands on himself he laid, and took
> An apostolic Chair:
> And then ordains his Creature Coke
> His heir and successor . . .

> It matter not, if Both are One,
> Or different in degree,
> For lo! ye see contained in John
> The whole Presbytery![10]

Provision of Services. The services John provided for the American church included ordination for deacon, elder, and superintendent. And he conferred on his superintendents the administrative and sacramental authority that was traditionally associated with bishops.[11]

But more important, the episcopacy of Methodism, even as it adapted to the democratic spirit of American life, did not relinquish or share the traditional right to ordain with others. Although eventually almost all administrative functions of a bishop could be delegated to the Annual Conference, ordination was reserved to the bishop alone. And in the rite for ordination of a deacon, Methodism retained the traditional practice in which only the bishop laid on hands.

Fluvanna Schism. Finally, there is an incident during the Revolutionary War when a group of Methodist preachers established a presbytery and ordained themselves presbyters. Asbury, in hiding at the time, finally prevailed upon them to desist from exercising these ordinations in sacramental ministry until a constitutional ordination could be provided. In Wesley's eyes, such ordinations were not valid. The situation was resolved in 1784 when Wesley ordained Coke superintendent and two of his preachers deacon and then presbyter for ministry in the United States. This long delay (when American Methodists were generally deprived of the Lord's Supper) only illustrates the lengths Wesley was prepared to go to provide a validly administered Eucharist.

Further Reflections on Ordination

What are we to make of the sequence of events that constituted the ministry of American Methodism? What implications do these events have for United Methodism today?

We can make several observations from what we have seen about Wesley's thought and practice:

(1) John Wesley held a high view of ordination, even after he loosened his viewpoint of the early church ministry.

(2) Only a bishop could ordain (he held himself to be a scriptural bishop in the theological sense of the early church). And even a bishop had to abide by the juridical decisions of the church. Sacramental ministry was not to be engaged in without ordination.

(3) Bishops are the same order as presbyters, but of a different grade.

(4) When Coke and Asbury assumed the title "bishop" (Wesley had called them "superintendents") Wesley objected vigorously. But his objection was based primarily on his fear of the public misunderstanding his overseers, since bishops were seen to be aristocrats in Britain. How could he, who had considered himself a scriptural *episkopos* for forty years, object to those ordained through him employing the common term for that office.[12]

(5) "Wesley did not mean that a bishop was only a presbyter, but that a presbyter was really a bishop, when he used episcopal functions. Wesley's ordinations were not in intention presbyterian, they were episcopal; they were given by a presbyter acting as a bishop; they were given by one who claimed to be, and for that reason gave them, a New Testament bishop." That is to say, he insisted on the *rite vocatus*, which meant, in the apt words of J. Bowmer, "No administration of the sacraments without ordination."[13]

AMERICAN EPISCOPACY

I have concentrated on Wesley's concept and exercise of episcopacy, primarily in his extraordinary ministry as it was exercised in Britain. Wesley's ministry laid the essential foundation of what became the Methodist style of episcopacy, and in many ways that foundation has remained intact in America.

In other ways, however, the superintendency Wesley exported to the American shores underwent important changes. The second half of this essay will be devoted to briefly illuminating the evolution of the office in the United States.

A number of major issues can be identified in which this evolution took place. Several of these points are: Relation of the bishop to the General Conference; Ordainer/appointer; Administrator; Prophet/priest; and Connection/itineracy. In a certain sense each of these categories affects the history and evolution of the episcopacy in Methodism in the nineteenth and twentieth centuries.

In 1784 Coke was ordained by Wesley. He came to America, and called a meeting of all the preachers. He told Asbury that Wesley wanted him (Coke) to ordain him as the second bishop. Asbury replied, "Well and good, but only if the preachers elect me." Here was a new kind of episcopacy, freely elected by the persons who were to serve under the authority of the new bishop. The preachers elected Asbury, and he was ordained deacon, presbyter, and bishop, on successive days.

In Asbury's *Journal* of the so-called Christmas Conference at which this took place, he wrote: "When the Conference was seated, Dr. Coke and myself were unanimously elected to the superintendency of the Church, and my ordination followed. . . ."

A *Discipline* was drawn up at the 1784 Conference; Section IV deals with the episcopacy:

Question 2:	How is the bishop to be constituted in the future?
Answer:	By the election of a majority of the conference, and the laying on of the hands of the bishop.
Question 3:	What is his duty?
Answer:	To preside as moderator in our conferences; to fix the appointments of the preachers for the several circuits; and in the intervals of the conference, to change, receive, or suspend preachers, as necessity may require; to travel through as many circuits as he can, and to direct in the spiritual business of the societies; as also to ordain bishops, elders, and deacons. . . .

| *Question 4:* | To whom is the bishop amenable for his conduct? |
| *Answer:* | To the conference, who have power to expel him for improper conduct, if they see it necessary. |

There are two interesting and relevant points in this first outline of Methodist episcopacy. First, the founding Conference of the church continued tradition by saying that the bishops would be ordaining other bishops and second, it was clear that this was a new kind of episcopacy, "amenable to the conference," and responsible to it for the conduct of the ministry.

Thus the American Methodist episcopacy was determined to be an episcopacy that the Christian church had not yet seen. Bishop John Nuelsen describes it well:

It is an episcopal form grafted into a presbyterian stem. The Methodists have never regarded their bishops in the same light in which the Episcopalians have regarded their bishops. Even Asbury said, "We make no special claim for the office of Bishop, as the Latin, Greek, English, or Lutheran bishops do. One can easily see, that we are so different, that we are not even third cousins." The office of bishop in the Methodist Church . . . does not belong to the essence of the church.[14]

In my opinion Bishop Nuelsen's observation is accurate. A basic shift had taken place in transplanting Wesley's British church organization to an American church, where bishops still exercised great power and authority, and did the same things Wesley had done, but in the context of the authority of a governing body to which they were amenable. Since 1784 other American church bodies, including the Episcopal church, have adopted similar patterns.

One of Methodism's great historians described the work of the new church's bishop in this manner:

He had extraordinary power, but also great amenability. He presided in Conference, made the appointments absolutely, and decided finally all appeals from both preachers and people. But he could be deposed and expelled from the church for "improper conduct," a liability to which no other preacher . . . was exposed. He had no higher salary than his ministerial brethren, he was allowed no local diocese, but must travel through the denomination.[15]

At least in the early years the way Coke and Asbury exercised their episcopacy may have corresponded to an early church apostolic, rather than episcopal ministry. They not only provided the eucharistic relationship among the growing number of congregations (gradually the presiding elder, and ordained preachers did also), but they gave great attention to preaching, helping to establish new societies, and mediating difficulties among the societies and congregations.

The authority of the Conference over the bishops steadily increased during the remainder of the 1780s—even the setting of dates had to get advance approval (the Baltimore Conference of 1787). In 1792, when the system of quadrennial General Conferences was put into place, the amenability of the bishops to the larger body was further increased. It was also at the 1792 General Conference that the first outright attack on episcopacy was made.

Further Evolution

It is well-known that Asbury's appointive authority was absolute, when appointments were made there was no appeal. This kind of authority (and his use of it) was soon resented, especially in a country that had just fought a war for freedom. A faction led by a preacher named O'Kelly argued for the right of appeal. When they lost they broke away from the church and formed the Republican Methodist Church.

The next significant development took place at the General Conference of 1808 when the church worked out and accepted what came to be regarded as its constitution. Included were a number of so-called "Restrictive Rules," which could be changed only with great difficulty. One of these, which had to do with episcopacy, stipulated: "They (General Conferences) shall not change or alter any part or rule of our government, so as to do away with episcopacy or destroy the plan of our itinerant general superintendency."

This rule has remained since 1808, and is regarded as the continuing anchor for United Methodist episcopacy, even though early in that same century the General Conference gave the bishops leave to plan their travel so they would not need to itinerate through the entire church as the first bishops did. We will note other changes as well. However, since 1808 the office has never been seriously challenged.

Nevertheless, the ideal (at least constitutionally) of the bishop being a general superintendent, and therefore able to travel throughout the connection (the denomination) remained effective in the mind and ethos of the church even when in 1816 and 1824, provisions were made for each bishop to concentrate service in one area.

This matter became intensely relevant in 1844 when a southern bishop inherited slaves through marriage. Northern delegates to the 1844 General Conference expressed the opinion that this encumbrance would make it impossible for him to itinerate to the northern conferences of the church, thus making his itinerating superintendency impossible. This was a basic constitutional reason for the breakup of the church into northern and southern parts. Even though the matter of each bishop itinerating throughout the church had already become academic, in this case it still had the potential to be a factor in the division of the church.

The ideal of a "general" superintendency of each bishop has continued into United Methodism (cf. Bishop Mathews' statement, pp. 149–150). This is true in spite of continuing evolution during the early part of this century, in which bishops were further restricted to serve in particular annual conferences and areas, and expected to reside in cities within their conferences. The principle of each being a general superintendent probably reminds the church of its Wesleyan, Asbury, or Otterbein roots.

Another innovation was the development of the so-called "missionary bishop." As foreign missions spread, the worldwide dimension of oversight needs became overwhelming. One solution the church experimented with was the missionary bishop. This person was elected to serve only in the area designated, not elected for life, as were bishops for the United States. Thus the principle of the 1808 Restrictive Rule was severely eroded; it was clear that all bishops were not created equal.

With the principle of localized episcopacy established by the acceptance of the missionary bishop, it was not long before bishops for these shores localized. In 1872 all bishops were asked to reside near certain key cities in the North, and between 1896 and 1912 they were gradually sent to particular areas—the appointment system extended even to the bishops. A kind of diocesan system began to grow, with the single provision that every bishop was still a bishop of the entire church, and that bishops move among areas.

Other innovations included the gradual granting of board and agency leadership and chairing to bishops. As these boards assumed greater powers, the possibility of chairing them gave the bishops great influence in the church. However, the traditional role of the bishops in the General Conference—without vote (and usually voice), but chairing the sessions—has continued until today.

Finally, as the divided Methodist churches prepared to reunite in 1939, one provision was the creation of a series of jurisdictions. The purpose was to regionalize the church in many respects. The election of bishops was also regionalized, moved from the General Conference, where they had been elected in a national forum, to these jurisdictional conferences, where they reflected and advocated more regional concerns. The 1968 union with the Evangelical United Brethren Church produced a change in episcopal administration when it voted to eliminate the Central (black, segregated) jurisdiction.

THE FUTURE

The disciplinary description of the ministry of bishop in the United Methodist Church was primarily administrative as late as 1976. Thus theologian J. Robert Nelson could write:

> The member of another episcopal-type church who reads the *Discipline* is no doubt disappointed in the total lack of any theological or historical warrant for episcopacy. . . . Nothing is said about the bishop's ministry as made familiar in recent ecumenical discussions of the office. Is the bishop *pastor pastorum?* Is the bishop a guardian of the faith "once delivered to the saints," and henceforth a teacher? Is the bishop a sacramental figure, a eucharistic leader? Does the bishop symbolize the unity of the whole church on earth?[16]

But a change is under way, probably caused by United Methodist contact with, and involvement in, the ecumenical movement. The more traditional experiences of, and responsibilities of episcopal leaders are having an impact on the United Methodist Church and its bishops. Thus the 1984 *Discipline*, in its description of the ministry of bishop, includes such paragraphs:

> Leadership—Spiritual and Temporal—1. To lead and oversee the spiritual and temporal affairs of the United Methodist Church, which confesses Jesus Christ as Lord and Savior, and particularly to lead the Church in its mission of witness and service in the world.
> 2. To travel through the connection at large as the Council of Bishops to implement strategy for the concerns of the Church.
> 3. To provide liaison and leadership in the quest for Christian unity in ministry, mission, and structure and in the search for strengthened relationships with other living faith communities.

4. To organize such Missions as shall have been authorized by the General Conference. . . .

Para. 515; To consecrate bishops, to ordain elders and deacons, to consecrate diaconal ministers. . . .

A movement toward a more traditional understanding of the ministry of bishop can be observed in these sentences.

This trend is more pronounced in the understanding of episcopacy, and in the commentary and prayers around the ministry of bishop found in the alternate *Ordinal* produced for the church in 1980. The presiding bishop says to those about to be consecrated:

My brothers and sisters,
You are to be consecrated
bishops in the Church of God . . .
All Christian ministry is Christ's ministry
of reconciling love.
All baptized Christians are called
to share this ministry of service in the world,
to the glory of God and for
the redemption of the human family.
From among the baptized
some are called by God and set apart by the Church
to serve God's people as deacons, elders, and bishops.
You have been ordained
to the ministry of Word and Sacrament;
you are now called
as a bishop in the Church,
to represent Christ's servanthood to the Church
in a special ministry of oversight.
You are called to guard
the faith, the unity, and the discipline
which are common to the whole Church,
and to oversee the Church's life and work,
and its mission throughout the world.
As a servant of the whole Church,
you are called to preach and teach
the truth of the Gospel to all God's people,
to lead them in worship,
in the celebration of the sacraments,
and in their mission of witness and service to the world.
As pastor to pastors,
you are to lead and guide
all ministers entrusted to your oversight,

join in the consecration of bishops,
ordain deacons and elders,
provide for the ministry of Word and Sacrament
in the congregations committed to your care,
and consecrate and commission other ministers
for service to the Church and to the world.
Your joy will be to follow the One
who came not to be served but to serve.

The traditional aspects of episcopal ministry emerge clearly in this statement, which helps explain how and why the United Methodist Church was able to affirm the May 1988 consensus document of the Consultation on Church Union (COCU), which in its general orientation of the ministry of bishop, contains such a description of episcopal ministry.

I will conclude by asking one question about the future of episcopacy and then several broader general questions.

The first question concerns the future of United Methodist episcopacy, a new ministry of bishops in a united Lutheran church, and for future reconciled relationships that, I trust, will eventuate between our two families. It has to do with a two- or a three-ordered ministry. What can be said on this subject in the context of United Methodist episcopacy?

In this essay I have made it clear that Wesley (eventually) and Methodism since Wesley, have held that the bishop is of the same order as the presbyter—the grade is different but the order is the same. Theologians throughout the history of the church, from Jerome to Thomas Aquinas agree.

But the terms of reference are changing. Currently the multilateral theological conversations (*Baptism, Eucharist and Ministry* [BEM] and COCU) agree that a threefold ministry should be the goal of the renewed and reconciled Christian ministry. It is obvious that these agreements refrain from using the traditional term "orders" for this threefold ordained ministry—there is too much historical baggage associated with the term "orders." The term "threefold (ordained) ministry" is being employed more often.

In the mid-1970s, when the World Council of Churches (WCC) published the interim results of its decade-long attempt to find agreement on the ordained ministry (which was the parent document of the BEM agreement), the United Methodist Church in the United States was asked to make an official response to this document. Representatives of the church (including theologians, pastors, and lay persons) were assembled by the Council of Bishops through the Division of Ecumenical and Interreligious Concerns. The following paragraph from this *Response* illustrates United Methodist openness on the question of orders.

We have emphasized that the episcopacy is not a third order, but presbyters are consecrated to that particular office. In the light of the COCU discussion, we realize with added force that our use of the name and office of bishop has not been totally in keeping with the usage in the wider tradition of Christianity and requires continued rethinking.[17]

Order or Ordering?

Our conception of "orders" has come to us through the Western part of the church, through Rome and Canterbury. Even in these churches the exact meaning of "order" has fluctuated and evolved through history. Even the eminent theologian Thomas Aquinas believed that the bishop shared the basic order of the priest, at least in its medieval setting.

But what about that setting? Perhaps the single most influential person in the development of the concept of "order" was Augustine, who in *De Civitate Dei* developed a highly "ordered" explanation of the structure of the world. "From Augustine was drawn in large part the consequent patristic and medieval emphasis on order, rooted in Neoplatonic thought. . . . In this view everything has its proper place . . . and the notion of the church as hierarchical is cast in the image of a multilevel society."[18] The concept was basic in Roman law.

Perhaps what needs to be questioned most today is why and how "order" and then "orders" was made normative in the church. The emerging ecclesiastical structure was rationalized and the result was "the elevation to the status of an intrinsically necessary and essential reality a structural evolution that was, at least to some extent, the result of human decision and specific social needs."[19]

Juridical notions of order are being called into question in today's ecumenical discussion, and emphasis is being placed more on a threefold ministry of diverse gifts and service. Therefore I would argue that Methodist churches can include their leaders within such a threefold ministry, stripped of traditional legalistic and hierarchical baggage. New understandings of Christian community, and the ways leadership in this community evolve and are authenticated, are being worked out in Methodist churches. Those of us who authorize and lay hands on bishops also recognize God's call and gifting, and invoke God's presence and grace in the bishop's ministry. Do we also understand this ministry as identifiable and accountable? The calling, function, and gifts of United Methodist bishops are different from those of the elder. Is not this what ordering meant in the early church? Can we recognize this difference once again?

Reinforcing the logic of this question is our present ambiguous use of two orders. American Methodists have gradually forgotten why the deacon should represent an order by itself; they behave as if the deacon is the introductory step to an elder's ordination. There is now, *de facto*, greater difference between the ministry of a bishop and an elder than there is between that of the elder and the deacon. Yet we claim that the bishop and elder are part of the same order, while the deacon and the elder are of different orders. We have not been consistent, or fully utilized the riches inherent in the concept of order.

Finally, scholars have noted that Asbury and Coke used the word "ordination" to describe the service by which they had been set apart to serve (as did Wesley himself). It should also be mentioned that in 1967 the Methodists in Great Britain felt comfortable using this term in the ordinal, *Toward Reconciliation*, that they prepared with the Church of England.

Possible Implications for United Methodists

If the United Methodist Church adopts a threefold ordained ministry as it accepts ecumenical agreements several results can be anticipated. For example, a shift to traditional ordination terminology will allow us to reemphasize, in a healthy fashion, some of the early responsibilities of the bishop. American United Methodism has maintained a feeling for the traditional roles of early bishops; usually Methodist bishops have been at the forefront of mission, and always at the center of ordination. In addition, United Methodist bishops have often led in the struggle for social justice.

Another possible result would be a serious questioning of Methodism's traditional itinerant episcopacy. Is this practice something helpful from a past era that we can leave behind, or is it something essential with which we must contend?

I believe that this question needs to be studied and debated. Therefore I would argue the former position. It is clear that Wesley's practice of constant itinerancy as the first Methodist superintendent was greatly influenced by the milieu. He felt the need to oversee (supervise) the whole, and only he could do it adequately. Methodism was a movement in the Church of England, and thus he could not and would not be settled in a diocese as the bishops of that church were. This made good sense for a movement within a national church.

But does it still? Methodism has made a principle of the itinerancy of bishops; until now many pastors remain in one congregation longer than bishops may stay in an area. Bishops need to be bishops of the entire church, who can function anywhere they are called. And they need to personify and embody the national and world church where they serve.

But I would suggest that in the future they need a longer and visible connection to the place they serve. Would not the church be enriched if each bishop could develop and maintain lasting relationships with pastors and congregations of their areas? The New Testament evidence we have, scanty as it is, calls for a more personal relationship of the bishops to their elders, as well as to their flocks. Traditionally the bishop has testified to the interrelationship of all congregations in one body of Christ; but for this symbol to be alive it is necessary that a bishop be able to visit the congregations and pastors frequently, to be able to listen to them, and interpret universal concerns for them. The New Testament exhortations concerning the focus of episcopal responsibility are always local. A more localized episcopacy would require more bishops, each overseeing fewer numbers of persons and having less staggering geographical responsibilities than present American United Methodist bishops.

Such localization would also give more attention to the organized mission of the congregation and Annual Conference. Once again ecumenical study has called attention to the church's responsibility to serve and sanctify the surrounding community and society. In order to do this, the church and its bishop need to be living parts of that society. Historically there has been a close relationship between the city and the bishop. How can a bishop who moves every eight or twelve years truly be a part of a city? Surely we can find a better symbol of the universal role of the bishop than this constant movement. Our pilgrimage from *ecclesiola in ecclesia* (in England) to *ecclesia*, to a more complete ecclesiological form of life in the future means taking the smaller diocesan patterns of episcopacy of the early church more seriously.

Does this mean giving up traditional Methodist episcopal concern for the whole? On the contrary, it means enlarging our concept of the whole. In the words of Professor John Deschner:

> The whole, for whose unity episcopacy is responsible, cannot be merely a denomination, but must be the whole community of God, both in its visible form as the one church of Jesus Christ, and in its latent form as "all persons of good will" . . . Hence ecumenical responsibility is the first responsibility of Christian bishops, and ecumenical recognizability is crucial to their office and authority.[20]

This enlargement of responsibility and recognizability is what the various agreements on ministry intend to accomplish. For these and similar reasons it is my conviction that the United Methodist Church would be best served by accepting and implementing a threefold ministry of deacon, presbyter, and bishop.

This last section may have represented an intra-Methodist discussion, but it has relevance for the United Methodist–Lutheran bilateral conversation. The uniting Lutheran churches will need to reach some agreement on this question among themselves, as well as in their conversations with Roman Catholics and the Episcopal church. And it is posed unavoidably for both of our communions in the BEM discussion, and for the United Methodists in the COCU future. It needs to occupy us at some point in this bilateral conversation.

I conclude with some general questions:

1. Both of our traditions, arising from the Reformation, put great emphasis on the rational, the understandable, and even the propositional. We understand the valid reasons for this direction, since we were reacting partially against a misuse of mystery. But what room do we leave for the movement and action of God's Spirit beyond our cognitive power or our intellectual categories?

This question has to do with ordination and the *epiklesis*. It also has to do with the person of the bishop. Is there something to the embodying, personifying *episkopé* that we can learn from and receive? Is not there value in a personal kind of community building, a eucharistic person ministering between the local congregation and the district or conference, that we need to examine carefully?

2. Sign/action: Can we say something together regarding the laying on of hands and the *epiklesis* that will be helpful to the ecumenical movement? In our histories we have both been suspicious regarding any manipulation of God.

68

How do we understand God's gifting in relation to human prayer in ordination? Has Orthodox theology something to give us that we have forgotten? What are we to make of the Pastorals late in the first or early in the second century, telling us about the stirring up of the gifts of the Spirit given through the laying on of hands?

3. Can we say something together about the apostolic tradition of the entire church? For example, in paragraph 34 of BEM we read that a large number of characteristics make up the apostolic tradition of the church, including missional and diaconal dimensions. Our histories have experienced this dimension of the apostolic tradition. Can we relate these truths to episcopacy in a helpful way?

4. Since we have no history of unchurching each other, is there some service our traditions could render by a mutual reconciliation of ministry (episcopacy) on a different model?

Could we help the reception of BEM by doing some conceptual work on the suggested reconciliation of ministries, since neither Methodists nor Lutherans put ultimate dependence on historic succession, and both denominations believe in succession through the ordination of presbyters?

PART THREE

THE PRESENT

3

The United Methodist Bishop and *The Book of Discipline*

THE POWER OF THE BISHOP

United Methodists are probably as diverse about what episcopacy means as they are on most other points of ecclesiology or theology. Perhaps it would be more accurate to say that many United Methodists have never really thought about it that much. For many United Methodist laypersons, the bishop becomes a reality only when a confrontation develops over whether their pastor should be moved or not. Then some laity are shocked to discover that an outsider has the power to make such a decision.

United Methodist clergy know a lot about bishops, but this may not be due so much to a consuming ecclesiological turn of mind as to the fact that bishops have a direct impact on where they live and what they do. A United Methodist preacher had better know something about bishops!

When we look to John Wesley, the founder of the Methodist movement, we see some ambivalence on this subject. Wesley believed that on the face of the earth there was no system of church governance more valid or truer to Scripture than that of the Church of England. Part of that system was the episcopacy, a third order of ordained ministry. Yet when the American Methodists took it upon themselves to start calling their two new superintendents, Coke and Asbury, by the title of bishop, Wesley was outraged, and wrote these famous words to Asbury:

How can you, how dare you, suffer yourself to be called Bishop? I shudder, I start at the very thought! Men may call me a knave or a fool, a rascal, a scoundrel, and I am content: But they shall never, by my consent, call me Bishop! For my sake, for God's sake, for Christ's sake, put a full end to this! Let the Presbyterians do what they please, but let the Methodists know their calling better. (Albert Outler, ed., *John Wesley* [New York: Oxford University Press, 1964], 25)

Why was Wesley so furious? He probably felt his child (American Methodism) was getting out of hand. Earlier in the same letter he reminds Asbury that while he (Asbury) is the elder brother of the American Methodists, he (Wesley) is the father of the whole family. And it may be because Wesley held the title "bishop" in such high regard that it hurt him so much to have a subordinate assume it.

But Wesley's harsh criticism did not deter the American Methodists from continuing to call Asbury "bishop," and the term soon became universally accepted. What was not accepted was the ecclesiological understanding of episcopacy as it functioned in the Church of England. American Methodism did not accept then, and it does not accept today, the idea that bishops are ordained to a third order of ministry. A person elected as a United Methodist bishop is not ordained into a different order of ministry, but is consecrated to an office, and continues to carry out sacerdotal functions as an ordained elder. Thus while a United Methodist bishop must be an ordained elder in order to be eligible to be named bishop (a matter clarified by our Judicial Council a few years ago), the bishop remains an elder as far as status in the church of God is concerned.

There are those who contend such ecclesiastical theory is rendered meaningless by our United Methodist practice of giving bishops life tenure. They say, "If you really mean that you're not changing their status, but are only asking them to fill an office, why don't you elect them for a term? Life tenure smacks of a status change, not just a functional change."

There is some validity to that argument, which can be answered only by saying that United Methodists apparently like it that way, or at least have not yet generated the political will to change it. If consistency were the hallmark of church polity, Lord who could stand?

No, United Methodist episcopacy is shaped by history and pragmatism, as are many other features of United Methodism. Let me identify and explain some of the characteristics of our episcopacy, and a rationale for each:

Characteristics of Episcopacy

Life Tenure. John Wesley was never a bishop in name, but he was in for life as the acknowledged leader of a religious movement.

Asbury followed that pattern in America, but only after insisting that he be elected by his colleagues. The early Methodist preachers assumed that they were electing their bishops for life and this unwritten practice continued. It was not until 1968 that life tenure was actually placed in our written constitution.

Life tenure continues today partly out of custom and tradition, but also for practical reasons related to a strong episcopacy. The church seems to be saying that it wants the continuity that goes with life tenure, and it wants bishops who are not tempering their actions and decisions because they have to worry about being re-elected. The church may also be saying that it needs bishops who are prepared to invest long-term time and energy into this task, which can result in a strong administration.

On the other hand, there are periodic efforts within the church to change from life to term tenure. Such a change would require a constitutional amendment, and seems unlikely in the foreseeable future.

Appointive Authority. United Methodist bishops, while constitutionally restricted in a variety of ways, still possess one very important power—that of appointing clergy.

This power originated with Wesley; as the undisputed leader of the Methodist societies, he appointed the preachers to their places untrammeled by notions of consultation with others. Asbury assumed the same authority; although it was challenged vigorously at times, and some schisms resulted, it remained intact.

The idea of a "bishop's cabinet" came into being about twenty or thirty years into our American history, where the presiding elders appointed by Asbury became a consulting body about making appointments. However, final authority remained with the bishop. It was not until 1916 that the General Conference legislated that a bishop must consult with the cabinet before making appointments. In 1928 the first provision for a Pastoral Relations Committee appeared in each local church whose purpose was consultation, and in 1976 such consultation became a requirement.

Until 1940 it was not even mandated that the minister had to be consulted before the appointment was made. A refinement of this came about in 1964. That year I was elected as a delegate to our General Conference, and assigned to the committee on the ministry. We had before us all matters dealing with ordained ministry. One day in a small sub-sub-committee we discussed this provision. One minister complained that in his conference the required consultation with a minister about to be moved might consist of a district superintendent saying to him, "We're thinking of sending you over to the other side of the state." Period. As a result, our sub-sub-committee drafted an amendment to *The Book of Discipline* that inserted the words "about his specific appointment" in the paragraph requiring consultation with the ministers. This was adopted by the subcommittee, the committee, and finally by the General Conference. Since 1964 it has been a part of our *Discipline.*

Constitutional Position. It is clear that the episcopacy is a constitutional office, rather than monarchical in character. Episcopacy could be abolished in the United Methodist Church, although it would take passage of a constitutional amendment to do so. This requires a two-thirds vote of the General Conference plus a two-thirds aggregate vote of all the members of Annual Conferences throughout the world. In the meantime, the General Conference retains authority to pass legislation regulating the episcopacy.

Itinerant Principle. Wesley's preachers were itinerant—not choosing their own place of ministry, or responding to a call from a particular congregation, but covenanting to go where Wesley sent them. This principle has continued to this day, although under increasing pressures due to changing social mores, working spouses, etc. But it should be noted that the bishops are also itinerant. They are not elected by the conference over which they preside, but by a larger regional conference, called a jurisdiction. Then they are assigned or appointed to serve in a particular location. Ordinarily they would be limited to serve no more than eight years in one place, with a possibility of extending that to twelve. But the itinerant principle governs their place of service in the same manner as all the rest of the ordained ministers.

Ecumenical Task. United Methodist bishops should approach their responsibilities ecumenically, because the constitution of our church defines us as but a part of the larger church of Jesus Christ. Most bishops take this very seriously and are committed to the ecumenical movement and its various expressions.

Administrative Position. Critics sometimes charge that we force our bishops to become only administrators at the expense of the pastoral role. There is some truth in this. For instance, the role of presiding at confirmation has never been assigned to our bishops and would seem to present practical impossibilities. To provide a diocesan episcopacy similar to the Episcopal church would require increasing our number of bishops tenfold or more. In the United Methodist

Church the district superintendent functions as a sort of suffragan bishop, and carries as much or more responsibility as diocesan bishops in some denominations.

Our peculiar nondiocesan system of episcopacy probably is closely related to the ministerial appointment system. A bishop needs to preside over a large enough body of ministers and churches to make itinerancy work.

Dual Role. Every United Methodist bishop is the resident bishop of a particular area, responsible for oversight and care of clergy and congregations in that place and also for clergy deployment there. But the bishop is also considered a general superintendent of the whole denomination, and in this capacity assumes some responsibility on various boards and agencies of the whole church. The hoped for strength in this dual role is an avoidance of parochialism on the one hand, but on the other hand a knowledge of what is happening in the grass roots of congregations that can inform the decisions made in national bodies.

The United Methodist episcopacy has its origins in the strong-willed, organization-oriented, energetic leader of a band of religious societies. This leader was a staunch believer in the historic episcopate, but did not hesitate, when occasion demanded, to take on episcopal functions himself, justifying this on the basis of Scripture. He was outraged when his American offspring started calling their leader by the title "bishop," but had no problem when they conferred on their leader powers considerably greater than those held by establishment bishops. No wonder the United Methodist episcopacy still reflects many of the contradictions evident in the life of Methodism's founder.

REGARDING THE UNITED METHODIST
BOOK OF DISCIPLINE

Throughout our dialogue, a constant reference point for the Lutherans was *The Book of Concord,* and for the United Methodists *The Book of Discipline.* The difference in these two sources of authority goes far toward explaining the Lutherans' and Methodists' differences in outlook regarding theology and ecclesiology.

Both groups look to Scripture as the authoritative standard for church life and work, but they appear to hold different views of how scriptural truth is revealed, interpreted, and lived out in the church. For Lutherans *The Book of Concord* appears to be a once-and-for-all authoritative guide for doing theology. For United Methodists, *The Book of Discipline* also provides an authoritative guide, but goes beyond theology to extensive pragmatic guidelines for the ongoing governance of the church. Furthermore, it is automatically up for revision every four years through its General Conference. Thus, the authority of these two books appears to be based on somewhat contrasting theories of revelation—*The Book of Concord* on a more static or final theory and *The Book of Discipline* on a theory of continuing revelation.

Having said this, let me add that it is never as simple as it may seem; differences of approach among pastors within the same denomination may rival those between the two denominations. With this in mind, let me attempt to describe the place of *The Book of Discipline* in the life of the United Methodist Church.

From 1812 or earlier in the Methodist Episcopal Church, the book was entitled "The Doctrines and Discipline [*Discipline* was printed in larger type than *Doctrines*] of the Methodist Episcopal Church." That title held for 128 years, with a continuation of twenty-eight years in the Methodist church. In 1968 the title *Book of Discipline* came into use.

What is significant is that from the beginning the emphasis was on discipline rather than doctrine. The book has always contained the Articles of Religion and other doctrinal statements, but within a larger context of the practical living and governing arrangements of the church. The Articles of Religion remain unchanged for over two hundred years, and in this sense they resemble *The Book of Concord*. But the majority of United Methodists do not look on the Articles of Religion as having the level of authority that Lutherans attribute to *The Book of Concord*.

Events at the 1988 United Methodist General Conference provide a good example of how United Methodists deal with doctrinal matters. The 1972 General Conference adopted a doctrinal statement that sought to give guidance in "doing theology." While it lifted up the primacy of Scripture, it also emphasized the so-called "Wesleyan quadrilateral" of Scripture, tradition, experience, and reason. It also made a point of theological pluralism as a value. This document, adopted overwhelmingly, served for sixteen years as a theological guideline for the United Methodists.

But over those years there developed a growing feeling that the statement did not adequately emphasize the primacy of Scripture, and that the emphasis on pluralism was being interpreted as a kind of theological indifference. In the face of this, the 1984 General Conference established a Commission to review the 1972 statement and bring recommendations to the 1988 General Conference. When the report of this body was released prior to the General Conference, it evoked considerable fear that the report went too far in giving Scripture heavy emphasis, and in seeming to discount the importance of tradition, experience, and reason. Delegates came to the General Conference with some fear of a major confrontation on these issues.

But in true conciliar (and pragmatic) fashion, the delegates in the Faith and Mission legislative committee faced these issues, struggled with them, and hammered out a compromise statement. This new statement was adopted overwhelmingly by the General Conference. Thus the unity of the church was maintained through the conciliar process.

Perhaps the great significance of *The Book of Discipline* for United Methodists is the fact that it is a living document that provides for ongoing opportunity for change to be effected. Hopefully such change comes about through sensitivity to the winds of God's Spirit. It must also be recognized that this constant opportunity for change involves the risk that the winds of political fads may be mistaken for the winds of the Spirit, but this risk goes with the notion of *The Book of Discipline* as a living document.

4

The Role
of the Lutheran Bishop

Materials on the bishop's roles come from three sources: Sacred Scriptures, Evangelical Lutheran Confessions (*The Book of Concord*), and synod constitutions with bylaws. All nine synods gave materials for this essay.

This study of bishops in nine Evangelical Lutheran synods includes 99.2 percent of United States' nine million Lutherans in eighteen synods. A lack of uniform polity, as the varied definitions of the following terms show, exemplified a Lutheran teaching: holy ministry is a service and not a system.

TERMS

Synod: A "synod" refers to a national U.S. Lutheran body.

District: A "district" is a region or nonregional part of a synod. Currently, two large synods have nonregional English or Slovak districts and one body uses the word "synod" for district.

Bishop: The American Lutheran Church (1970), the Lutheran Church in America (1980), and the Association of Evangelical Lutheran Churches (1980) adopted the title "bishop" for their regional and national leaders. The use of the term "bishop" was optional in the American Lutheran Church. Today, 63 percent of Lutherans (the ELCA) have bishops. We follow them and use the term "bishop." In this study bishops are referred to with masculine pronouns; at this time there are no female Lutheran bishops. However the ELCA decided the Sacred Scriptures allows women to be pastors and bishops (cf. Gal. 3:28; 1 Cor. 14:34–35; 1 Tim. 2:11–15).

The title "bishop" was long avoided by Lutherans in the U.S. for two reasons: Sacred Scriptures and history. The Sacred Scriptures use *episcopos* in 1 Tim. 3:2, 8, for bishop. It is also used in Scripture to mean presbyter, pastor, and elder. Titus installed presbyters as bishops (Titus 1:5–7). Paul refers to himself as apostle, not presbyter or pastor. Peter says he is copresbyter, shepherd, pastor (1 Pet. 5:1, 2). John is presbyter in 2 John 1, 3 John 1. In Phil. 1:1, Paul mentions deacons and bishops. Paul speaks of presbyters and bishops in Acts 20:17, 28.

Lutheran pastors fulfill the role of bishop in their local congregations—they take the role seriously. Until recently, Lutherans avoided the term "bishop" because of the negative connotation it had from the 1600s. Early bishops embarrassed Lutheran bodies by using their power to lord over their synods.

UNDERSTANDING THE TERM "BISHOP"

Episcopos, the New Testament–LXX Greek and Latin (Hebrew PKD), means "bishop," a word assimilated into Anglo-Saxon as *bisceop, biscop.* By 1150 A.D. it became *bisceop, bisop,* or bishop.

Episcopé does not mean "be lord." In Genesis 41 Pharaoh "set Joseph over all the land of Egypt" (not *episcopeo* but *kathistemi*). The LXX, translated "be lord" as "take over," "conduct," "set apart" or in Acts 7:10 "appointed." Jesus condemned lordship (Mark 10:42–44). Peter tells elders not to exercise lordship (*katakurieuo*) over those in your charge (*kleros*). So, resist lordship (1 Pet. 5:1–3).

We can see why the church adapted *episcopos* for oversight when examining the LXX and the New Testament usage of the word.

To be *episcopos* is when God appoints Joshua (Num. 27:16–19) or Moses assigns (Num. 4:27, 32). Leaders attend or tend flocks (Jer. 23:2). Elihu accuses Job of saying God does not greatly heed transgression (Job 35:15) but in *episcopé* God does care (Deut. 11:12), examine facts, and note results (Exod. 3:16).

An overseer watches over flocks (Acts 20:28), but Judas held the position of watching over finances (Acts 1:20). Paul says, "Keep watch over yourselves and over all the flock of which the Holy Spirit has made you overseers to shepherd the church of God" (Acts 20:28). Jesus replenishes his ministry after Judas (Acts 1:17–26). Someone who oversees must have a firm grasp of the Word (Titus 1:9).

An overseer minds his own assignment and is no mischief maker (1 Pet. 4:15). He makes judgments (Num. 16:29), observes suffering (Exod. 3:16), and diligently seeks the flock's peace (Heb. 12:15).

Inspectors of work are *episcopoi* (Num. 4:16). Army officers are *episcopoi* (Num. 31:14; 2 Kings 11:15). Overseers investigate complaints (Num. 16:29), look after a charge (2 Chr. 24:6), keep faith (Isa. 23:17), and dispense God's grace (Heb. 12:15).

An overseer ordains, setting others apart (Num. 27:16–19). He oversees work (Neh. 1:9; 2 Chr. 34:12, 13; 1 Pet. 2:25). He preserves people in the faith (Heb. 12:15), performs noble tasks and performs tasks nobly (1 Tim. 3:1–5).

In distress an overseer protects and aids (Heb. 12:15), seeks out those who hurt and are in need (Ezek. 34:11). With regard he reviews work (Neh. 7:1–2) but does not lord it over those in his charge (1 Pet. 5:3).

To advance God's Word, he searches for good workers (Acts 6:3), desires to see everything as God would see it (Job 20:29), and shepherds God's flock (Acts 20:28).

He silences opponents (Titus 1:11), is a steward of God's ministries (1 Cor. 4:1), and strengthens believers (Titus 1:9). He studies (Exod. 3:16) and surveys situations (Deut. 11:12; Ps. 27:4). He aptly teaches (1 Tim. 3:2). He visits (Luke 19:44; Exod. 3:16) with mercy or judgment (Gen. 50:24; Job 35:15; 1 Pet. 2:12) and is known as a witness of Jesus' resurrection (Acts 1:17–26).

As the previous Scripture references reveal, the bishop's multidimensional role is revealed throughout the Bible by the varied uses of the word *episcopos*.

THE OFFICE OF THE BISHOP

Some Lutherans view bishops as apostolic, sent away on an (*apostolleo*) unending divine mission. Preceding the noun apostolic was the action verb *apostolleo*. Titles are first a function, then they are given to the performer. *Episcopeo* preceded "overseer," *poimaino* preceded "shepherd," and *diakoneo* preceded "servant."

The apostle Paul was commissioned, went forth, preached, and evangelized. Concerned about the teaching, doctrine, and the teachers (Gal. 1:1), as well as the Pastorals, he oversaw his helpers. He healed and spoke in tongues, all *charismata*, all administrations of bishops, but neither he himself nor others in the Sacred Scriptures title him bishop.

Workers differ, so do assignments and functions, but all are gifts from God. To administer is a charisma, a favor bestowed. An overseer's (administrator) function is a favor from God, as is healer, miracle worker, teacher, and user of glossolalia (1 Cor. 12:28–30). He who desires to be a bishop desires a "noble task" (1 Tim. 3:1). An apostle, prophet, pastor with concern is gifted.

A bishop is a servant, gifted with what is called a "pastoral" approach. "The man cares." Pastors, not administrators, make good bishops. They live *episcopé*. A bishop cares as the shepherd who risks leaving ninety-nine to seek one lost—checking for the absent and weak, searching for and attending the needy. He gathers, not scatters, looking after a flock with regard and concern.

A bishop uses this special caring gift to oversee as God does, to examine himself and his work, to review and check to see what happens. He visits with mercy or judgment; when seeing a need he considers how to fill it, and boldly appoints or assigns.

A bishop visits, investigates, examines, inspects, studies, looks diligently at work and workers. He will not agree to drop the issue, but silences opponents of gospel ministry—surveying to protect the workers and strengthen them in their task. He teaches that Christ is alive and caring.

The role of *episcopos* is not ranked as an order or a ministry level, but is a service, neither superior nor separated. A bishop functions where assigned. He does not wander in churches in search of a place to rest, but exercises oversight where called.

A synod bishop respects district bishops and does not thwart their work. A district bishop respects and does not pry into a pastor's work. When flaws or weaknesses appear to hinder gospel proclamation, an overseer supervises the pastor.

A bishop, as all other believers, is a steward of God's mysteries (1 Cor. 4). The gospel, centered in Christ's message of grace, is the "glorious gospel of the blessed God" (1 Tim. 1:11), the "power of God for salvation" (Rom. 1:16). It is the glory of all his servants, whether apostle, prophet, evangelist, pastor, or bishop (Gal 6:14).

WHY DO LUTHERANS HAVE BISHOPS?

The Lutheran church can survive without bishops. The gift of oversight can be provided in other ways, by a pastor, by a committee of parishes, by one selected neighboring pastor. But the church needs holy ministry.

This gospel ministry is *primum mobile* for a bishop. This is a theological not an anthropological fact. The church is not a corporate structure, but incorporation in Christ. It does not seek an authority but a ministry authoritative in God.

God's grace requires no human oversight to have an effect. The Holy Spirit operates freely and cannot be under regulation. Messengers require regulations to encourage faithful ministry. A Lutheran bishop finds it difficult to resolve an issue with a human handbook instead of the divine Book; to use bylaws to ask for ministry emphasizing grace; to be presidential and work with rules, threats, plea bargains, and church-authorized procedures. This is true whether he uses divine counsel or human arrangements for marital counseling, alcoholic programs, or educational leave. Filled with the Spirit, the bishop seeks to be pastoral. Evangelical Lutherans cringe at authoritarian bishops. Polls show pastors, especially those under fifty years of age, prefer bishops who are pastoral not administrative.

Proclamation needs the holy ministry (Romans 10; 2 Cor. 5), but Sacred Scriptures assert that Christ's gospel does not depend on human ministry or human effort. We are saved by God's grace through the vicarious atonement of Jesus Christ.

"So faith comes from what is heard, and what is heard, comes through the word of Christ" (Rom. 10:17). "But how are they to call on one in whom they have not believed? And how are they to believe in one of whom they have never heard? And how are they to hear without someone to proclaim him. And how are they to proclaim him unless they are sent? As it is written 'How beautiful are the feet of those who bring good news!' " (Rom. 10:14–15).

All this is from God, who reconciled us to himself through Christ, and has given us the ministry of reconciliation; that is, in Christ God was reconciling the world to himself, not counting their trespasses against them, and entrusting the message of reconciliation to us. So we are ambassadors for Christ, since God is making his appeal through us; we entreat you on behalf of Christ, be reconciled to God (2 Cor. 5:18–20).

The bishop aids a messenger in doing a task. God is a God of peace (1 Cor. 14:33). He calls us to live in peace (1 Cor. 7:15). Order and peace in ministry find support through a bishop.

In the Old Testament Moses heeded Jethro's counsel to share his task, so people regain peace and harmony (Exod. 18:13–27). In the New Testament the apostles needed help to spend more time promoting God's Word (Acts 6:1–7). Both Moses and the apostles shared the work. Christ's body works best when members share, assist, and participate. Jesus advised that each has his own work (Mark 13:34).

A bishop, however, does more than share or transfer a pastoral responsibility. As an overseer of a pastor's parish, he aids or assists a pastor in working better.

Positive results come from oversight. Fellow pastors in need of aid find a bishop/overseer helpful in moving elsewhere for renewal, or staying and working out problems. Criticism can help by promoting self-growth. Many parishes appreciate a bishop's guidance and direction in helping to fill an empty pulpit. Dissenters applaud a bishop's support in resolving a difficulty. A bishop oversees to examine and encourage spiritual life growth for parishes and pastors.

A bishop also handles abuses to or by pastors. Doctrinal aberrations are corrected. Parishes are revived and apathy overcome. Comfort is given to pastors who hurt. Ministerial candidates are encouraged and recruitment appeal is answered.

As with all ministries, a bishop is subject to abuse, corruption, self-elevation, political intrigue, and constant temptation to make his area an order, a jurisdiction apart, an authority level to control others with prudence or expediency.

Our foe Satan, is loose in the church. The devil roams and devours. Church workers fall prey to divorce, alcoholism, unbelief, doubt, drug dependency, and public offense through self-desire and temptations. A bishop's call to repent along with absolution provides the church with new joy in ministry. Churches rejoice and thank God for a bishop who cares.

Today's ministry is not easy with society's problems in race or family, rivalries (inter-Lutheran or interparish), apathy or disinterest. A bishop usually settles problems on the lowest level. He boldly admonishes parishes who steal others' sheep. He encourages new churches to open, while offering needed forgiveness, hope, and courage to old ones in closure.

His most difficult task is helping to remove guilt and barriers that keep someone from remaining in holy ministry when the person could serve God better out of it.

A bishop uses his time and spiritual stamina to search for good workers to aid committees. His goal is that many obtain faith in Christ, and that the faithful remain faithful.

A Limited Ministry

The bishop's area of oversight is limited to an assigned place. The manner of and extent of oversight comes from his synod's constitution and his pastoral heart. A bishop's ministry has a *kleros*, a lot, an assignment, as had Paul, Peter, and Judas (Gal. 2:7, 8; Acts 1:17, 20, 26). Limitations, area, and time are good restrictions. Constant elections are a human method to bishop the bishop. All caretakers need to be taken care of. The bishop's office, restricted and administrative in practice, hinders him from a full Word and Sacrament ministry. The occupant needs release from the "house of lords" stigma and "the leprosy of leadership" phenomenon.

A bishop's ministry needs to be in Word and Sacrament. The bishop detests services that unordained servants could do and longs for pastoral services. A famous synod journal pictured its bishop far from home baptizing his grandchild. The caption read, "Bishops, too, baptize." A bishop ought to be required to return to a parish so as a pastor he can once again find that pastoral joy.

De Jure Divino or De Jure Humano?

Bishop is not mentioned as a gift in office or in service to the church (Eph. 4:11), although it is a gift used as a form of assistance, a form of leadership (1 Cor. 12:28).

Sacred Scriptures list qualifications for any in oversight (1 Tim. 3, Titus 1). A minister chosen as a bishop, is ordained or set apart by the church (1 Tim. 5:22). His call is rooted in Christ. His role is more than being able to function and preach the gospel and administer sacraments (Matt. 28, Mark 16). His call is to function, perform, do, and act. A pastor who is able to visit parishioners but does not, is unfaithful. If he is called to preach and celebrate, condemn false doctrine, and knows what the Word teaches (Titus 1:9), then he ought to teach (1 Tim. 3:2; 5:17; Titus 1:9) and witness (Acts 1:17–25). Oversight is only a part of his ministry. As a bishop, he is to aid and assist the pastors and parishes. He is to demonstrate what the plural of *kubernesis* (administrate, 1 Cor. 12:28 NIV) means, "those with gifts of administration."

The bishop finds joy knowing Christ as an exemplary *poimen*, shepherd, and *episcopos*, guardian of souls (1 Pet. 2:25), an arch bishop (1 Pet. 5:4), who will give the humble bishop a "crown of glory that never fades away."

A bishop's office is *de jure humano*. Christ's body initiated the special office, also deacons (Acts 6), church delegates of Corinth (1 Cor. 16:3, 4), or Jerusalem's Council, (Acts 15:22, 25). God approved and supported a church's choice of a traveling companion for Paul (2 Cor. 8:19). The episcopal office is of human origin (2 Cor. 8:4).

A bishop supports Lutheran educational institutions in his region. He encourages support of a district auxiliary, charity, camp, seminary, college, social ministry, and mission work.

A bishop is elected by congregational delegates to assure all parishes of their elections for ministry by ordination or installation rites, even if these may be done by a pastor. Scripture makes no demand for a parish or clergyperson to join a synod, nor for a synod to have bishops; yet all Lutheran synods require a bishop's approval for clergy installation. By such human *episcopé*, synods assure parish and personnel of a synod's support for a parish's mission commitment and a synod's care and concern for all personnel in ministry—local, regional, or national.

Congregations do not elect a bishop as they do a pastor, but uninstructed delegates elect. There is no proportional representation or quota system of delegates in the vote. Once elected, a bishop retains his ministry (service) status, until he loses the election and is rescued for parish ministry, or retires when his bishop status ceases.

THE ROLE OF THE BISHOP AND ITS PRESUPPOSITIONS

The following presuppositions affect a bishop's work:

(A) He confesses justification by grace through faith on account of Christ as central in Sacred Scriptures and our Confessions as a guide in proclamation and administration.

(B) Having the office of the keys he affirms the priesthood of all believers and gives spiritual sacrifices to gather people out of darkness into light. This is a *modus operandi* for carrying out his own work.

(C) He daily searches God's Word, knowing no other guide or direction. As a Lutheran he does not trust in visions, church synods, or councils. Thus he can better evaluate ecclesiastical teaching and life with *sola scriptura*.

(D) He is ordained, set apart for God. By his election he vows to follow all church regulations, to maintain a gospel ministry that is not covered by or opposed by God's Word.

He maintains a relationship with his Lord and diligently exercises the privilege of keeping in touch with the Lord, whom he expects to face and hear say, "faithful over a few . . . now ruler over many."

THE ROLE OF THE BISHOP AND ADDITIONAL ADMINISTRATIONS

The bishop appoints conference delegates, journal editors, members to fill vacancies on committees or boards, all of which he is ex officio member. He is involved in the conferences district workers arrange; there he reports the actions of the synod and district.

The board of directors adds more burdens on the bishop, for example, in finance campaigns. Constitutions require that he censure in the doctrinal arena, supervise personnel, work with executive staff, and be involved in all special synodical drives and concerns.

The bishop arranges conventions; he appoints essayists, worship leaders, preachers, chairpersons, and members of committees. He chairs sessions, gives recommendations, and reports to delegates. He approves advisory delegations. He prepares agendas and final reports with the district secretary.

The district bishop maintains the roster of workers. In some synods this is the work of the synod's bishop or secretary.

Through a special assistant a bishop is often responsible for parochial schools and staffs. He serves on regents of schools, colleges, and seminaries. He aids in the selection of professors and in establishing policies.

The Council of District Bishops meets to support the synod bishop and at times shares administrative concerns. Some synods use theological commissions or faculties to issue statements of belief or practice; other synods desire the Council of Bishops to be more vocal as the official teaching office of synod because of Sacred Scriptures (Eph. 4, 1 Tim. 3:2).

THE BISHOP'S ROLE WITH PERSONNEL IS BROTHER TO BROTHER

A variety of work and workers requires a bishop's oversight: Campus ministries; candidates of varied ministries; chaplains of hospitals, jails, armed forces; colloquies and their placements; deaconesses; directors of education, youth or music; dismissal of workers; discipline cases; externs, interns, vicars; interim pastors; mission developers; new workers; graduate placements; reinstatements of those who were dismissed or resigned; social ministry workers; worker priests, teachers of congregational schools and seminars. A bishop works with various congregations, subsidized or self-supporting, special or multiple.

As far as the bishop's personal status is concerned, he has full congregation membership. He may serve as parish assistant, but his main work is in his district. The synod bishop is a congregation member as well as a district member where he resides. No bishop is removed from fellow-pastor collegial relations.

The district bishop finds collegiality with other district bishops and the synod's bishop. He is the district's chief executive officer if there is an interdistrict conflict of mission or personnel.

The synod bishop strives for collegiality with other Christian leaders, especially other Lutheran synods. He directs dialogues to discuss matters that disturb or divide.

The bishop is concerned about the church's image before the public, but his greater desire is caring for his people, his pastors and their people, his congregations and their spiritual life. He cares with obedience to his Lord and Savior Jesus Christ, following Luke 10:16, "Whoever listens to you listens to me." He endeavors to let those words be true in his teaching, visitation, and all his work of oversight.

5

Authority in the Church:
A Lutheran Perspective

The church most simply defined "is holy believers and lambs who hear the voice of their Shepherd." (Smalcald Articles III, xii). Luther was right on target with the Scriptures with this totally artless, ingenuous explication of the church's boundaries, the faithful fold of believers, among whom there can be no pseudo-sheep. The Chief Shepherd, the Lord Jesus Christ, knows without fail who are his (John 10:27–29; 11:51f.; 15:6; Rom. 8:9; 1 Cor. 3:16f.; Eph. 1:22–23; 5:23–27; 1 John 2:19). In his famous treatise of 1539, On the Councils and the Church, Luther makes the point that even a seven-year-old child knows this truth.

Thus the true nature of the church has to do with people. Christ is the church's only Head and Sovereign. By its nature the church is a spiritual community traversing all time and place. No secular relationship (family, race, or nation), mere external connection, fellowship around given rites or external objects, but personal faith alone makes people members of Christ, and of Christ's mystical body and church.

What Christians confess in the Creed, "*Credo-unam, sanctam, catholicam et apostolicam Ecclesiam,*" is true in every point because of what Christ has done for his church. It is one, numerically and in unity of faith and hope; it is holy through the perfect, imputed righteousness of Christ; it is catholic because it embraces all believers; it is apostolic because it is built on apostolic teaching.

Christ, the Bridegroom, has given all the powers and privileges which belong to his beloved, the church. These are the church's treasures. The church is the royal priesthood of which Scripture speaks. No hierarchy, individual, church body or synod, mediates between the royal priests and Christ. Christian believers come boldly into his presence with all their petitions and spiritual sacrifices completely confident of his mercy. The keys of Christ's kingdom, Word and Sacraments, are this royal priesthood's possessions to use and proclaim. They are not vested in a special order of priests, clergy, church bodies, popes, or bishops.

Christ builds his church. He does so with his Word, by the gospel of forgiveness through his atoning sacrifice that is to be proclaimed in all the world for sinners' sakes. Thus the Word, along with Baptism and the Lord's Supper, becomes the mark of the church's presence upon earth. The Word is never preached in vain, but by his promise it will accomplish the purpose for which he sent it. The gatherings of believers that cluster around the Word are not accidental. It is the Lord's will that congregations, called churches in the New Testament because of the believers present there, assemble all those who profess faith in Christ for worship, prayer, instruction, godly discipline, and fellowship at the Lord's Table.

Local churches exist by divine will. The keys belong to them. The relation of local churches with the *una sancta*, the holy Christian church of all believers, is coextensive as regards membership. Christ does not have two churches, although it is appropriate to speak of the invisible nature of the universal church at the same time that one speaks of the visible Christian church on earth. Thus there are not two charters. Whatever powers and privileges Christ has endowed the *una sancta*, he has vested the local congregation in fullest measure.

The ministry of the Word, therefore, belongs first of all to all believers, not to a special class. Every Christian congregation has this responsibility from the Lord. Included in these powers and duties is the need to call a qualified pastor. This is God's will, and ministry in the narrow sense, referring to the public pastoral office, exists *jure divino*, by God's institution. Congregation and pastor exist in correlative relationship, the pastor performing publicly the things that belong to all the royal priests. The pastor comes into office by the call of the congregation, through which by Christ's command the powers of office are delegated.

Luther saw no conflict between these two articles, the sovereignty of the royal priesthood and the God-ordained pastoral office. They formed a wonderful ellipse that Christ himself set up for his church, like two poles around which the life of the church moves in God-intended symmetry and function.

Assisting Christ's Mission

Associations or groupings of congregations into larger bodies may be a godly and beneficial arrangement. In fact, New Testament paradigm points the way toward cultivating a wider fellowship of sister-churches, banded together for mutual strengthening and joint church work. The Scriptures are silent on the form that such bodies should take and on whether they should be thought of as prescribed or commanded. Although they serve a useful purpose, there is no ground to the claim that God requires them, or to any pretension that apostolicity has been given to any person or set of persons to rule or govern over them, as in the so-called historic episcopate.

It is true that the unity of the church universal, the *una sancta*, ought to have its counterpart in the visible Christian church. Division and schism in the latter is contrary to God's will, as is the vaunted pluralism of Christian bodies. These splits trouble all Christians. We strive and pray that such disruptions be overcome. But fellowship in the faith rests upon true unity in belief. Such bond only results from fidelity to Christ's Word, not from fabricated ecclesial structures that are built upon minimal formulas of union.

Fundamental to Lutheran theology is the recognition that the church in this world cannot create anything to enhance the nature of Christ's church, which he creates whole and perfect. Synods of congregations may be formed, but they do not *ipso facto* advance Christ's kingdom. They are voluntary organizations that exist *jure humano* and must always be seen as such. They are representative churches, which bear the name "church" in a representative fashion, by virtue of certain powers or functions delegated to them by the member congregations. They exercise no overlordship over and above the congregations, but are super-ordinated only to the extent that given functions have been delegated to them by the congregations they represent. The church work they do belongs first of all and fundamentally to the congregations they serve. The congregations, through the instrument of a synod, cooperate in doing the church's work by preparing qualified persons for the public ministry; but the congregation's individualism remains intact.

As far as the internal affairs of congregations go synods have advisory powers only, not legislative. At the same time each congregation, as a member of the *ecclesia representativa* or *concordita*, values the fellowship and unity that it has within the synodical body, cooperates fully in the joint mission, and fosters the fraternal spirit by joining in the proclamation of the gospel with kindred minds. The congregation does not derive its powers from a super-church, by whatever name it is called, but from Christ, who bestows the keys of the kingdom upon every community of believers. It was in America, under the First Amendment guarantee, that Lutheran congregations first had the freedom to establish, or set in operation, the principles Luther articulated at the time of the Reformation opposing Rome's hierarchial concept of the church and ministry—individual churches, or congregations, were free from government and/or consistorial domination in religious matters. C. F. W. Walther, pressed by controversy over these issues in his own circles and guided by intense study of Scripture and Luther's writings, was able to throw off the old state-church yoke and articulate clearly the fundamental principles that characterize Lutheran thinking and practice on church and ministry. The constitution of the church body that Walther helped to found carefully delimited the synod's authority:

> In its relation to its members the Synod is not an ecclesiastical government exercising legislative or coercive powers, and with respect to the individual congregation's right of self-government it is but an advisory body. Accordingly, no resolution of the Synod imposing anything upon the individual congregation is of binding force if it is not in accordance with the Word of God or if it appears to be inexpedient (*ungeeignet* in the original) as far as the condition of a congregation is concerned. (Art. VII on Relation of the Synod to Its Members)[1]
>
> Motivation for forming a synodical union was twofold:
> 1. The example of the apostolic church in Acts 15:1–31.
> 2. Our Lord's will that the diversities of gifts should be for the common profit in 1 Cor. 12:4–31.

Fundamental to this bond of stated purposes was the unequivocal pledge to hold to the articles of Christian belief taught by Holy Scriptures and the Lutheran Confessions, as contained in *The Book of Concord*.

The congregations remain the basic units within the synod, which, in turn, is seen as an extension of these congregations, as are the various geographical districts and circuits. Through these structures the congregations exercise stated functions as agreed upon in the delegate synods, which meet regularly for that purpose. The officers elected at such general synods serve in accordance with the duties assigned to them and remain accountable to the congregations who, along with their called pastors, constitute the synod.

The right of judging and deciding all matters, including doctrinal, is shared by all members of the royal priesthood, pastors and laity alike. This principle was first clearly articulated by Luther. He reminded the church that Christ's admonition to guard against false prophets in sheep's clothing was spoken as much to the pew as to the pulpit, in fact first of all to the pew. "The laymen," stated Walther, "are entitled to sit and vote together with the pastors in ecclesiastical courts and councils," and to judge in doctrinal matters (Thesis X, *Church and Ministry*). All such judgments must conform and be subject to Scripture's teaching. The right of private judgment does not entitle anyone to sit in judgment over Scripture, which Luther firmly contended is its own interpreter, *Scriptura interpres sui*, or *Scriptura Scripturam interpretatur*.

While every Christian is obligated, as a baptized follower of the Lord, to speak and witness for the Word of God, it does not follow from this that each believer holds the public pastoral office. Scripture requires that there be special aptitude to preach and teach beyond the ability of the average Christian, and also that a person possess a valid call from the congregation of believers to minister the Word and Sacraments publicly. It is such a call that empowers the pastor for office and, as Luther pointed out, focuses labors on a given field of labor at that place, to preach, teach, render care, administer the sacraments, exercise Christian discipline, and evangelize the unchurched. Holy Scripture speaks directly to the necessary requisites for the pastoral ministry (Titus 1:9; 1 Tim. 1:19; 3:2, 7; Titus 1:6), and it becomes the duty of the congregations to require that these qualifications be met. A pastor becomes unfit for office when found unfaithful to God's Word and the Lutheran Confessions, or persists in willful misconduct.

The importance of the congregation's call of a qualified person into the pastoral office is seen also in the relation of that call to ordination. Luther points out that the former is necessary by divine injunction on the basis of Scripture; the latter (ordination) is a desirable usage with roots deeply set in *apostolico-ecclesial* practice or ordinance. It is a solemn ratifying of the call and earnest petitioning by all the priests for God's blessings upon the ordinand and the congregation a pastor is called to serve. Ordination does not confer the ministry. The call and its acceptance make the minister. Ill health or incapacity can be reasons for resignation from the ministry. Luther's point is that ordination does not confer a kind of indelible character.

The power of the ministry is the power of the Word. All, people and pastors alike, give it unconditional obedience. It is because of the Word and the office that the royal priests dutifully honor, respect, and love their pastor. However, in matters that are not addressed or taught by God's Word, there can be no binding of consciences.

Before God and the Word there are no superiors or inferiors in the church, not in the station of ministers in relation to congregations, or between the incumbents of the pastoral ranks. Executive positions and grades of supervisory officials within the church, particularly in the *ecclesia representativa,* or synod (church body), are of human origin. Whatever titles or functions are assigned to these ranks remain human arrangements and may be altered or discontinued as necessary.

Bishops in the apostolic church were ministers in charge of local congregations and also called elders. There were no bishops in the diocesan sense. The office of supervising bishop was a later addition in the church and generally acknowledged to be a human right only. It was virtually equivalent to superintendent, or president, in synodical polity. Even Luther noted that there was no basis to the notion that the episcopal office was self-perpetuating, conferred from one who has the office to another aspiring for it. In many instances the people's consent bestowed the office. Nor was a bishop's consecration required for the vesting of office. Thus Luther installed his friend and colleague Nicolaus von Amsdorf as bishop of Naumburg.

The office of pastor is the one divinely instituted office in the church. Properly speaking, therefore, that individual is a pastor who is the pastor of a congregation. Other offices that may be found necessary for the church's well-being are auxiliary to that chief office and, following apostolic precedent, lie within the area of Christian liberty, either within a congregation or in a synod (church body). Such offices are created and governed by the congregations constituting the synod, deriving their importance and functions in that way for the performance of joint work, programs, and counsel. On the local level there may be teachers (parochial school), assistant pastors, elders, and councilmen; on a national level, synodical officials, professors, various governing board executives, etc. All of these offices exist for the sake of the churches and their ministry of the Word. Such auxiliary offices may cease, depending upon circumstances; but the churches or congregations may not dispense with the office of the called pastor. There is no substitute for the pastoral office; it is the highest office in the church by virtue of its divine ordaining.

Elected executives in the *ecclesia representativa*—bishops, presidents, supervisors, and other officials—have served the church well and efficiently. It is unlikely that they will ever be discontinued, as little chance as the synods themselves. Constituting congregations, however, always need to be on guard against power that overreaches given limits. Human pretension and pride are always around the corner, creating episcopal offices (officers) that vaunt themselves over the royal priests, attaching to themselves titles, dress, and airs that clash with the Master's and apostolic example and word. The organizations and stations that men create in the name of the church and Christ must serve him and the gospel, not self-serving ambition or pretension, especially not at the expense of "holy believers, lambs who hear the voice of their Shepherd."

Thus ultimate authority in the church remains with the Shepherd, Christ, who vests upon his fold, the church, royal prerogatives and responsibilities for the ministering of the Word and Sacraments. It is by God's ordaining that the royal priesthood of believers has the authority and power to issue a divine call to a qualified (1 Tim. 3, 1ff.; Titus 1, 5ff.) person into the pastoral office to do the things Christ has entrusted to the church.

PART FOUR

POSSIBLE
FUTURES

6

Reviewing and Reforming the Episcopacy: Ecumenical Resources and the United Methodist Episcopacy

As heirs of the reformation, Protestants appropriately ask about the accountable exercise of the episcopal office. Given the concerns about abuse of authority, a dialogue between representatives of two Protestant communions must ask how accountability is maintained for those in the episcopal office. I will examine the way the episcopacy is operating presently in the United Methodist Church. This case study will hopefully prove useful for a similar process concerning the diverse developments within Lutheranism. Principles for patterning and practicing ministries appearing in *The COCU Consensus* and the WCC's convergence on BEM[1] will guide in this analysis.

These principles do not only help in reviewing current practices, but help in exploring ways to reform the episcopacy in order that there will be a responsible exercise of the office for unity in the church's mission.[2] This paper begins with a summary of the guiding principles, and then employs them in reviewing current practices and explores possibilities for renewing the episcopacy in the United Methodist Church.

PRINCIPLES FOR PATTERNING AND PRACTICING MINISTRIES

According to the guiding principles, ministry of laity and ordained persons is to be "personal," "collegial," "communal," and "constitutional."[3]

Personal Principle

The exercise of ministry is personal because "in every minister, lay and ordained, Christ and the Gospel are made present as personal reality and are the source of that life of holiness and devotion which is a mark of ministry."[4] Such a principle says an individual takes responsibility for exercising whatever ministry that person is given. The individual, lay or ordained minister, must reflect the life of Christ and the gospel we proclaim.

Collegial Principle

The practice of ministry is also guided by a collegial principle as individuals "associate . . . with others who share the same call."[5] Within a given group of ministers, lay or ordained, persons share responsibilities in a collegial body. While "collegiality" is not used explicitly, the word implies mutual accountability among those who share membership in the same group—laypersons, deacons, presbyters, and bishops.

Communal Principle

As the collegial principle expects a calling will be shared within a particular group, the communal principle calls for "intimate relations between the different ministries." This principle sees each of the distinct ministries "rooted in the life of the worshiping and witnessing congregation and (thus requiring) the local church's effective participation in the discovery of God's will and guidance of the Spirit."[6] By highlighting decision making in the community, BEM expresses the contribution of the laity, deacons, presbyters, and bishops in curbing the excesses in the hierarchical modes of governance associated with the episcopacy (see the *Commentary to BEM* 26).

Constitutional Principle

I have been considering the material principles by suggesting that ministry is patterned and practiced personally, collegially, and communally. In addition there is a formal principle that is constitutional. To explain that ministry is ordered and operates constitutionally is to say that the specific understandings of the three principles are more than a policy foisted on the body by an individual (e.g., a charismatic figure) or a group in power at a given time. The constitutional principle must also be more than a tacit agreement or policies developed by chance. The constitutional principle provides policies and procedures that are duly adopted with mutual consent of the various parties involved—laity, deacons, presbyters, and bishops.[7]

BEM is concerned about the constitutional or canonical status of all three of the previous principles because they represent historic and valid polities that have emerged in various communions—the episcopal polity with its emphasis on the personal principle, the presbyterial with the collegial, and the congregational with the communal.[8] In other words, the constitutional principle will legally or canonically order the household of faith with contributions from each of the polities that the ecumenical convergences have uncovered as valid for reforming ministries in a church uniting for mission. Although no single tradition has had the capacity of embodying the full range of principles and polities, BEM looks forward to their presence in the body of Christ.

In reviewing these principles, the implications for exercising the episcopacy have been apparent. I will review current practices in the United Methodist Church and explore ways these principles may suggest that the episcopacy could be reformed for the church's unity in mission.

REVIEWING AND REFORMING THE UNITED METHODIST EPISCOPACY

Personal Principle

The Book of Discipline[9] spells out the personal responsibilities of a bishop at two points. The first appears in a list of "Specific Responsibilities of Bishops" for which they are personally accountable. The responsibilities are classified under three headings: Leadership (par. 514), Presidential Duties (par. 515), and Working with Ministers (par. 516). The second list of personal responsibilities appears in the section on "The Nature of Superintending" (pars. 501–502). The word "superintending" is the historic word for exercising "oversight" or *episcopé*, paralleling "supervision" which appears more frequently in Lutheran documents.[10] The second list (par. 502) includes a description of the "Mode," "Pace," and "Skill" the denomination expects from the "general superintendent" (bishop).

In addition a bishop takes public vows in the service of consecration. The *Discipline* has nothing to say, however, about the status of the pledges made to expectations that appear in the Order of Consecrating a Bishop. Not all pledges come directly from the *Discipline*.

These considerations highlight what the person does in the office or in an official capacity and less to do with the person in the office. In the sections dealing with the episcopacy, the *Discipline* emphasizes what a person does in the office, but says less about who the person is. Accountability has more to do with the position than the person, gifts than graces.

We may mitigate this issue by saying that a bishop remains an elder in the church and that the qualifications for ordination as elder (par. 431) still apply. The expectations are far more explicitly personal. An elder is expected to

1. have personal faith in Christ and be committed to him as Savior and Lord.
2. nurture and cultivate spiritual disciplines and patterns of holiness.
3. be aware of a call by God to give themselves completely to their ministry, accepting God's call to be his servant.
4. be committed to and engage in leading ministry of the whole Church in loving service to humankind.
5. be able to give evidence of the possession of gifts, graces, and promise of future usefulness.
6. be willing to make a complete dedication of himself/herself to the highest ideals of the Christian life; and to this end agree to exercise responsible self-control by personal habits conducive to bodily health, mental and emotional maturity, fidelity in marriage and celibacy in singleness, social responsibility, and growth in grace and knowledge and love of God.
7. be persons in whom the community can place trust and confidence.
8. be competent in the disciplines of Scripture, theology, church history, and church polity, and in the understanding and practice of the art of community and human relations.
9. be accountable to The United Methodist Church, accept its *Discipline* and authority, abide by the demands of the special relationship of its ordained ministers, and be faithful to their vows as ordained ministers of the Church of God. (Par. 431)[11]

While the understanding of the denomination is that as elders these personal qualifications continue to apply, the fact that they appear in another section besides the one dealing directly with bishops weakens the continuing applicability of these personal responsibilities. The personal principle of patterning and practicing the ministry of a bishop could be strengthened in the United Methodist Church if the *Discipline* stated explicitly that the vows assumed for membership in the church, and the vows for ordination to the order of deacons and elders continue to be applicable. In this way, accountability for being a particular person in the office as well as faithful exercise of the episcopal office would be heightened.

Collegial Principle

The collegial principle operates in various settings for bishops in the United Methodist Church: Cabinets, Colleges, a Council, a Conference, the Committee on Investigation, and the Court for Trial.

Cabinets. Collegiality appears most immediately in the cabinet where district superintendents (pars. 520–524) are seen as "an extension of the general superintendency," or the episcopacy (517). As such, we can say the general descriptions concerning oversight apply to this forum (pars. 501, 514–516, 529–533).

The collegial principle appears in the appointive work of the cabinet. Bishop and district superintendents are required to consult elders whom they appoint (par. 531). Parity and mutuality appear in the open itineracy policy, meaning that "appointments are made without regard to race, ethnic origin, sex, color, or age" (pars. 530, see also 4, 506.2, 517). Unlike any other elders, the *Discipline* stipulates a tenure that bishops and district superintendents can serve in a particular place (par. 518). Bishops are called "itinerant general superintendency" (par. 17).

College. Bishops are organized into colleges within various geographic regions (par. 51). Their functions are not stated and their activities vary considerably. The growing regionalization of the denomination could mean a strengthening of the colleges. It is in this setting that bishops beginning in the episcopacy designate another bishop as something reminiscent of a Counseling Elder (par. 411), or clustering of elders in the Annual Conferences "to encourage the building of peer groups among the clergy for mutual support and discipline; to build systems of mutual support for clergy families" (par. 522.3).

Council. Upon their election, bishops become members of the Council of Bishops (par. 527). "The Council of Bishops is . . . the collegial expression of the episcopal leadership in the Church and through the Church into the world" (par. 527.2). Collegiality is expressed as the Council speaks "to the Church and from the Church to the world" and provides the denomination "leadership in the quest for Christian unity and interreligious relationships" (par. 527.2). The Council is expected to develop collegiality with "other councils and service agencies of the Church," as it fulfills "its oversight of spiritual and temporal affairs" of the whole church (par. 527.3).

Conference. United Methodist bishops maintain ties with affiliated autonomous or united churches. Both groups were previously Methodists or from another associated parent body but now belong to an independent Methodist or united church. The denomination authorizes quadrennial meetings of the bishops or executives of these related bodies as stated in the *Discipline,* although the agenda of the meetings is not specified (par. 528).

Committee and Court. Like other professions as well as groups within the church, the denomination provides for collegiality at certain stages in the disciplinary actions of its own members. Although the communal principle operates in the review stages in handling the grievances and complaints (pars. 513.3–.5) against bishops, as revealed in the next section, the investigation of charges and trial of members function with a collegial principle. Elders as peers or colleagues of bishops constitute the committee investigating charges (par 2623.2) and the court conducting the trial of bishops (par. 2624.2c).

In reviewing the collegial principle, I noted a failure to articulate functions for the College of Bishops and the Conference of Methodist Bishops. Growing regionalization within the denomination and the growing interaction with the global outreach of the denomination through its own connections and ecumenical involvements suggest that the denomination needs clearer expectations from these collegial relationships. This is important if we are concerned about the church's unity in mission.

The mandate for the Council of Bishops calls for much more reform than the authorized promulgating of pronouncements and promoting of ecumenical ties that occur at Council meetings. United Methodist bishops could spend more time in study and renewal during the Council meetings, following the purpose for gathering bishops in the Evangelical Lutheran Church of America.

I have spoken of the Cabinet as an illustration of the collegial principle, but it may be more accurate to speak of a collegial mode in making appointment with a communal principle in patterning ministries. The work may be collegial among elders who are peers, yet in the end the episcopal office bears the responsibilities for decisions differently than district superintendents, suggesting that the communal principle is finally operative. Other practices in the denomination raise a fundamental question about the actual status of bishops in relation to other elders. Are they a separate order or pattern of ministry, or are they the same order in a different office? The denomination could be helped by further reflection on this point.

Communal Principle

Bishops are not an entity unto themselves. They exist and operate communally in innumerable ways. Given the number of instances, it will be possible to focus on only two types of communal settings.

Communal Context for the Episcopacy. The episcopacy emerges out of the life of the community. While we may speak of the episcopacy as a gift from God in terms of the Holy Spirit's guidance of the church through history unfolding *episcopé*,[12] it is still valid to see *episcopé* as an expression of the life of the church as a human community. First, there is the theological understanding that bishops are part of the people of God, even if they are a distinct expression of the one ministry of the church as revealed by God in Jesus Christ and empowered by the Holy Spirit. The theological substance of this viewpoint appears in the treatment of ministry in the *Discipline*. In dealing with "The Ministry of All Christians," it begins with a section on "The Heart of Christian Ministry" that is based on the revelation in Jesus Christ, then moves to the "General Ministry of All Christian Believers," and finally to the "Representative Ministry" including the diaconal and ordained. Hence the ministry of bishops is placed within the ministry of all Christians which is patterned after Christ.

There is also a practical expression of this basic understanding. Laypersons and ordained clergy, select (par. 506), appoint (par. 507), support (pars, 623, 735), and review (par. 513) bishops. They also serve in a committee for appeals (pars. 2601, 2625.2). The presence of bishops within the church is determined on the basis of the communal principle.

Communal Operations of the Episcopacy. The work of bishops with other groups is vividly illustrated in the presidential duties (par. 515), in legislative procedures (par. 515.1), and liturgical practices (par. 515.4). Similar functions also appear in boards and agencies (par. 805), also in the investigations (par. 2623.2) and trial (e.g., par. 2624.1b) of lay and clergy where they convene, constitute, and preside.

Several lines of reform come to mind in reviewing the United Methodist episcopacy. First, United Methodists could affirm more explicitly their view that bishops are a part of the body of Christ. This would strengthen the basis for unity within the church for mission. The COCU model of beginning the description of each pattern of ministry by anchoring it in baptism offers a promising model.[13]

United Methodists could also strengthen the priestly role of the episcopacy. The current emphasis on administrative leadership, presiding roles, and appointive processes (pars. 514–516), could be supplemented with clearly defined roles in the sacramental life of the church and as one who leads the people of God in prayer at key moments.[14] The prophetic role of the office could be strengthened equally with a Christology in "The Ministry of All Christians" (*Discipline*, pars. 101–110) comparable to the one found in *COCU Consensus* (secs. 1–20), especially in the way COCU moves from Christ's redemptive work (secs. 2–4) to Christ's reconciling acts (secs. 5–9). Such a theological foundation could lay groundwork for greater global unity for mission.

Constitutional Principle

From this case study's constant references to the United Methodist *Discipline*, it is obvious how theory and practice are legally or canonically ordered. There may be unwritten practices that continue, but at many key points they are agreements established in duly constituted bodies.

The Wesleyan strand of the denomination came out of the eighteenth-century British ethos that produced the social contract theory. It is not surprising that the eighteenth-century forebears adhered to their religious practices by documenting their contracts, canons, constitutions, and covenants. In other words, the constitutional principle is obvious in articulating the understandings and practices of the episcopacy in the United Methodist Church.

The BEM convergence invites us to explore "the consequence (we) can draw from this text for (our) relations and dialogues with other churches" (BEM Preface).

THE REFORM OF EPISCOPACY

Several conclusions come to mind. First, the four principles for patterning and practicing ministry in COCU and BEM have served the descriptive and prescriptive steps we have followed in this continuing quest to reform the episcopacy for unifying the church in faithful mission. Of the many contributions of COCU and BEM, the four principles could become one of twentieth-century ecumenism's significant contributions for understanding ministry.

Second, this analysis has revealed that the four principles have been operating in the United Methodist episcopacy.

Third, this does not mean that the exercise of the office is immune from abuse. Something more is needed. In other words, while the personal, collegial, and communal principles are "material" and the constitutional principle is "formal," the church still needs a "substantial" principle to guide us in developing the contents of the principles concretely. The Reformation tradition of the Word of God offers substantive suggestions. The Word appears in its written form as Scriptures. Come, Holy Spirit, our hearts inspire! The living expression of the Word of God comes to us in Jesus Christ, the Servant as Lord and the Lord as Servant. Come, Lord Jesus! Amen.

7

Episcopacy as
Point of Unity

The ministry of bishop in the Christian church has been understood as the fostering of unity among the presbyters, deacons, and laity. How has this ministry of unity been exercised in the Methodist tradition?

The following pages note how the bishop has helped maintain the unity of the movement and church as a minister of the sacraments, leader in mission, and general superintendent.

In order to glimpse the whole picture, time is spent sketching how the ministry of bishops has occasionally been a source of disagreement and even divisiveness in the Methodist tradition.

If this bilateral work on the ministry of bishop is to have lasting value, it is very important to study traditional points of division in episcopal ministry, and articulate a vision of future episcopal ministry that will truly help to enable both the mission of the church to the world, and the manifestation of the unity God has given us in Christ.

UNITY IN THE SACRAMENTS

As with many things Methodist, the question of episcopacy as a point of unity needs to begin with the life and ministry of John Wesley, the first acknowledged bishop and archbishop of Methodism. Wesley's oversight was unquestionably the center of unity for the entire movement as long as he lived. For most of his life he planned, directed, and occupied center stage in the Methodist movement throughout the British Isles like a military general (with whom he was sometimes compared).

Although he compared himself with a scriptural *episkopos*,[1] (and thus felt he had a right to ordain when circumstances demanded it), his episcopal oversight within the Methodist movement had an interesting similarity to the way episcopacy, as an identifiable ministry, emerged in the early church.

It is now generally agreed that, historically speaking, first-century bishops and presbyters were people exercising the same ministry, in different parts of the church, called by differing names, depending on the geographical and religious background. By the early second century so-called monepiscopacy was emerging, with bishops beginning to assume responsibility for intercongregational relationships.[2] Wesley knew about, and claimed as precedent, this early parity of presbyter and bishop; he cited it as justification for his right as a presbyter to ordain. And as a priest of the Church of England, when new societies and classes sprang up as the result of his preaching, he would naturally serve the Holy Communion to those groups as a qualified presbyter. But as the number of societies increased, he spent more of his time traveling among these para-church groups, building his connection, and overseeing it as its first *de facto* bishop. So from the beginning, the *episkopé* Wesley exercised in Methodism had to do with the sacraments.

Another aspect of Wesley's oversight in the episcopal sense had to do with his eventual ordaining of presbyters. This development has been rehearsed elsewhere in this book. But we need to remember how closely he connected ordination with the authority to administer the Lord's Supper. One example suffices: When several of his preachers in the New World formed a presbytery and ordained themselves (before he began to ordain), Asbury (at Wesley's behest) requested them to desist until Wesley could provide ordained persons. Thus during the entire Revolutionary War Methodists in the colonies did not have access to the sacraments—all because of the close bind with which Wesley tied ordination (by a scriptural *episkopos*), and presiding at the sacraments.

John Wesley did not discuss any theological reasons for his practice in his writing and speaking. It undoubtedly sprang from the discipline of the Church of England, which inherited this tie between episcopal ordination and permission and empowerment to administer the sacraments. But his practice of oversight held to an inseparable connection between ordination (and thus the bishop) and sacramental unity. He never considered his followers to be out of communion with the Church of England; in his own presbyteral/episcopal person, the connection had been maintained.

Wesley's position has been continued throughout the history of Methodism. It is the bishop (in succession from Wesley) who ordains presbyters and deacons; bishops consecrate other bishops. The church has not really supported succession, however Methodism has maintained its own succession in uninterrupted fashion.

An important point should be noted: Wesley had learned to differentiate between the power of order and jurisdiction in his reading of Bishop Stillingfleet's work entitled *Irenicum*, published in 1659. Stillingfleet had distinguished between the power of order to exercise ministry and sacraments, as presbyters do, and the power of jurisdiction which is in the hands of those appointed by the church to lead, such as bishops.[3] Although Methodism continues to insist that its episcopacy is of the same order as its presbyterate, in jurisdiction the bishop is an entirely different ministry.

In Methodism the bishop has, since the time of Wesley, served as a point of sacramental unity in the authority to ordain. No one else ordains. Along with the deacon, only the bishop lays on hands. Further, thus far in Methodism's history, only ministers of Word and Sacrament (that is, ordained elders) have been elected to the ministry of bishop. James Mathews describes the background:

> Wesley's dilemma was a fierce one; either course he could take offended his High Churchmanship deeply: leave his people without sacraments or have an open break with the church. He solved the dilemma, for the Americans at any rate, by making provision for a threefold ministry of deacon, elder, and superintendent, thus effectively providing for a *church* for Methodists there.[4]

Ecumenical agreements in descriptions of the ministry of bishop in a reconciled ministry state that bishops have a responsibility for maintaining the apostolicity and unity of the worship and sacramental life of the church.[5] It appears that in their capacity as ordaining ministers, the bishops of Methodism have exercised that ministry in the traditional sense.

Having looked at the sacramental dimension of the ministry of unity of bishops in the Methodist tradition, it is necessary to mention one aspect of ministry closely related to the sacramental, in which the superintendents of Methodism have not provided a uniting ministry. This has to do with the spiritual dimension.

The COCU Consensus suggests that it is important for bishops to be shepherds to other ordained ministers, to "further the spiritual unity of their areas," to be available in as wide a range of personal relationships as possible.[6] The episcopal office in Methodism has not been notable for its success in this kind of availability to congregations or to pastors, due probably to its modeling of Wesley's own oversight. The *pastor pastorum* aspect of episcopacy has suffered in Methodism, partly because of the tremendous size of conferences and areas, partly because of the administrative overload placed on bishops' desks. Individual bishops who were so inclined could find ways of pastoring, but both the expectation of the church and the description of the office of bishop made the fostering of spiritual unity difficult.

The manner in which the United Methodist *Discipline* describes the ministry of the superintendent illustrates the point I am making:

> From apostolic times, certain ordained persons have been entrusted with the particular tasks of superintending. Those who superintend carry primary responsibility for ordering the life of the Church. It is their task to enable the gathered Church to worship and to evangelize faithfully.
>
> It is also their task to facilitate the initiation of structures and strategies for the equipping of Christian people for service in the Church and in the world. . . .[7]

Ordering seems to be the overall category, but worship is high on the list within that broader description. Another area of primary significance is mission.

UNITY IN MISSION

The quote from the 1984 *Discipline* of the United Methodist Church reminds the reader of the continuing high priority of the *missio dei* in United Methodism: "to enable the gathered church to worship and evangelize faithfully." These two dimensions of Christian discipleship were never separated by John Wesley. In fact, one vital reason behind the birth of Methodism was the need to stress both.

As Wesley had served as apostolic father of the early Methodist movement in the provision of an episcopal ministry that took seriously the ordering of sacramental life, he also served as a true apostle in the sense of being sent out to preach the good news. There are few Christians in history who expended more energy or

111

effort in witnessing, by word and deed, to God's mighty act in Christ.

As first bishop of the movement, and as primary mission strategist, Wesley held as inseparable true *episkopé* and the fostering and care for mission. The bishops of Methodism were so bound up with mission and the attached traveling and concerns that they could have been accused of neglecting many other aspects of traditional episcopal ministry until about the beginning of the twentieth century. Here was an episcopal oversight virtually defined by the needs of mission, from the 250,000 miles traveled by Wesley, to an equal number traveled by Asbury on a wild frontier, to Coke who crossed the Atlantic eighteen times, and died on his way to establish a mission in Ceylon.

As numbers and area grew, the decisions made were never to stop episcopal traveling, but only to become more efficient in travel: who, where, and when? And when, at the end of the nineteenth century, the church directed its bishops to focus their energy on particular geographical areas, the reason given was not to cease their missional labors, but to concentrate and intensify them into manageable areas.

Bishops, as centers of unity in mission, also have to do with a continuing aspect of United Methodist ministry that others have difficulty understanding—the appointive power of United Methodist bishops.

From the beginning of Wesley's movement, this kind of appointment to fields of labor has characterized it. Wesley put it boldly: if people wanted to come and work with (for) him, they needed to expect that he would appoint them where and when to go. He knew the entire system better than anyone else, and could best match needs and talents. Such matching, and covenanted obedience, were vital factors in the ability of Methodism to deploy ministry in response to need and opportunity. Rapid growth was one result. And since there was relative equity in remuneration, and all were expected to move regularly, there was fairness (and thus satisfaction) with the system. This pattern continued in the New World until approximately the time of the Civil War, when a settled pastoral ministry began to evolve, which posed new problems and suggested new styles of episcopal ministry.

GENERAL SUPERINTENDENCY

Methodist thinking and practice through the generations have emphasized that bishops in this tradition are general superintendents, not diocesan bishops. In the early years, bishops patterned their ministry on that of Wesley, traveling "through the whole connection," holding conferences, overseeing the work of the church wherever they went.

When this practice became unwieldy, or wasteful, fields of concentration were agreed to, and eventually assigned. But the church, and the bishops, still held to the theological point that each is a bishop of the entire church, able to minister anywhere they would be called to serve.

Bishop James Mathews, in his recent book on episcopacy, puts it strongly:

> Though our obligation to our assigned areas is of fundamental importance, it does not relieve any of us from a responsibility for the whole Church. . . . The general superintendency is not exercised merely, or even mainly, by the individual bishops but chiefly by the Council as a whole.[8]

Bishop Mathews makes a great deal of this general superintendency, calling it a joint itinerant general superintendency, one superintendency for the whole church, shared equally by all the bishops.[9] Bishops are not diocesan officers; they are charged with general oversight and "promotion of the temporal and spiritual interests of the whole Church." Bishop Mathews traces this view back to Ignatius and Cyprian.[10]

Perhaps this insistence on a general oversight reveals that the original pattern of Wesleyan superintendency was based on the apostolic model of Paul. Thus Asbury could say, "We . . . try sacredly to maintain our traveling plan and support a true missionary apostolic church."

The basic point is that United Methodist bishops are charged collectively with the temporal and spiritual interests of the entire church. This can, however, be stated in a way that raises questions. For example, Bishop Mathews writes: "Each of them and all of them are bishops of the entire church and pastors of all the parts; wherever one bishop is, the whole of episcopacy is there in his or her person."[11]

Such a statement seems to approach the fullness theory of Vatican II, in which the bishop comprehends all of the other ministries. Bishop Mathews's thesis is accurate: general superintendency is a powerful symbol of the unity of the church.

SERVANTS OF UNITY

Bishops of Methodism have, from the beginning, exercised a ministry seeking unity with other Christians and churches. Wesley never stopped his search for unity with the Church of England, Asbury sought and established relationships with Otterbein and Boehm, asking Otterbein, for example, to lay on hands at his (Asbury's) ordination.

Coke did his part in this succession by trying (unilaterally and unsuccessfully) to interest early Episcopalians to reconcile the ministries of the two churches. He also offered to submit to the laying on of hands.[12]

Ecumenical agreements put the ministry of servant of unity as a crucial aspect of the ministry of bishop.[13] Bishops of the separated Methodist churches were among the leaders in starting the long pilgrimage toward the reunion of the three churches, and they have been among the leaders in the founding and support of the World Council of Churches (WCC), the National Council of Churches (NCC), and the Consultation on Church Union (COCU). Furthermore, the Council of Bishops serves as a corporate ecumenical office of the United Methodist Church, in addition to the professional staff employed to facilitate such work. That responsibility is stated in this manner:

> In formal relations with other churches and/or ecclesial bodies, the Council of Bishops shall be the primary liaison for the United Methodist Church. The secretary of the Council of Bishops shall be responsible for these relationships . . .[14]

The role of the Council is significant. Thus in 1986, the official response of the United Methodist Church to the WCC *Baptism, Eucharist and Ministry* (BEM) agreement was submitted to the Council of Bishops for study, discussion, revision, and communication to Geneva. An official task force had produced a sixty-page document on this subject after eighteen months of work, and the General Commission on Unity of the church had produced its own document for submission to the bishops. The bishops insisted on studying the document carefully and revising it before approving the text.

Another area of episcopal life and work that may be affected by ecumenical agreement is the traditional responsibility of the bishop to be a "teacher of the apostolic faith." *The COCU Consensus* puts it this way:

> Bishops have a responsibility, corporately and individually, to guard, transmit, teach, and proclaim the apostolic faith as it is expressed in Scriptures and Tradition, and, as they are led and endowed by the Spirit, to interpret that faith evangelically and prophetically in the contemporary world.[15]

This area is attracting more attention and interest in the United Methodist Church. In an address to the Council of Bishops in April 1986, Professor John Deschner elicited some audible "Amens" from the bishops when he encouraged them to seek greater responsibility in the teaching ministry.

The issue is crucial: What are the implications of the priesthood of all believers to the magisterium of the church? Does participatory democracy, as it works in general assemblies of denominations today, serve as an adequate instrument of discerning the apostolic faith, through the Holy Spirit? Can the bishops of the church regain this ancient responsibility, and exercise it in a new way, involving the expertise of the *laos* in their work, so that history and the future can be related in an authentic and obedient manner? Do recent pastoral letters show us a way?

A POINT OF DIVISIVENESS?

One cannot write responsibly on the subject of episcopacy as a point of unity without making at least a passing reference to the place that church bishops have played in dividing the church through the centuries. Without describing that role in Orthodox or Roman Catholic controversies, we should, in this bilateral conversation, remember the point made some years ago by Joseph Burgess in a study paper—that it was difficult to find any Roman Catholic bishop who was faithful to the gospel in the years of Luther's challenge, or in Hitler's era.[16]

The same can be said regarding the slow separation of the Methodists from the Church of England in Britain during the years 1744–1784. Wesley tried to enlist episcopal interest or support for his work many times; he applied more than once for ordination of some of his preachers. The bishops were unanimous in their rejection until very late in his life, when the movement had acquired a momentum and life of its own. This is relayed simply to point out that through the centuries bishops have probably failed as often as they have succeeded in being apostolic teachers, reconcilers, or agents of unity. Thus it can be said that the bishops of the church have often been a point of divisiveness, if not division.

This fearful generalization continued in Methodism as well, though perhaps for different reasons. Methodist bishops became centers of contention in the American Methodist Church for reasons that had more to do with their style of oversight, their sometimes dictatorial concern to keep the troops circulating effectively on an expanding frontier.

Schisms that rent the church in 1792 and 1830 were, in part, occasioned by disagreements as to how Methodist bishops were leading the church. Although slavery was the primary issue in the division of the church in 1844, the person and *episkopé* of bishops was also very influential. Through the first third of the nineteenth century, the churches of the South gradually became strict constructionists of the constitution of the church, giving their bishops continuing and great autonomy to govern (read rule) the church. During the same years the conferences of the North became broad constructionists, giving more and more authority to the General Conference, at the expense of episcopal power. Thus the North could effectively challenge an unacceptable bishop to limit his episcopal administration. At that time there was no Judicial Council to adjudicate the matter, and separation was the result.

In recent years episcopal leadership has continued to concern the church, but in a less divisive manner. For example, in the 1970s there was a movement to bring into being a "term episcopacy," as had existed in the Evangelical United Brethren Church. The General Conference of 1976 did not accept this change. But that issue is still alive. Individual bishops seem to feel that their role is continuing to be "whittled away" in the church. Thus Bishop Mathews writes:

> We have seen repeated efforts to erode the necessary authority of general superintendents that makes this system effective. A whittling away at the episcopacy continues. The *Discipline* makes clear that episcopacy is itself intended to be a regulated and accountable body.[17]

EPISCOPACY AND THE BISHOP

The dual nature of United Methodist episcopacy—general superintendency and responsibility for a specific episcopal area—actually

116

reinforces unity in the church. The United Methodist bishop is at the focal point between the worshiping congregation and the national manifestation of the church. Constant attention to local church problems helps bishops keep their national and global commitments in touch with reality. Their involvement on the national and global levels helps them avoid provincialism.

Thus it can be said, as BEM suggests, that United Methodist bishops "relate the Christian community in their area to the wider Church, and the universal Church to their community." Furthermore, they are also "representative pastoral ministers of oversight, continuity and unity in the Church."[18] Their effectiveness in some of these dimensions can be improved, but the ecumenical discussion is making us more sensitive to the traditional values of this ministry.

As various ministries are reconciled and function as one ministry, it may be hoped that some of the values of Methodist exercise of episcopacy may find a way into the episcopacies of other traditions.

8

Bishops as Points of Unity and Continuity

The Ministry section of BEM states that bishops are to be "representative pastoral ministers of oversight, continuity and unity" (sec. 29).[1] Why? What reasons can be given for seeing in the episcopacy a point at which the unity and continuity of the church are especially focused? This essay develops an argument for such a focus. I will not argue that any particular form of episcopacy is either necessary or sufficient for the church's unity and continuity. The goal is to show episcopacy as an appropriate means and sign of the church's unity and continuity. The argument seeks to support the sort of episcopacy proposals found in BEM, *The COCU Consensus*,[2] and *Facing Unity*.[3]

My argument proceeds from three judgments about the nature of ministry and episcopacy.

1. The ordained ministry, that is, the ministry of Word and Sacrament or of Word, Sacrament, and order, is constitutive for the life and unity of the church.
2. That ministry has a collegial character.
3. The oversight of ordained ministry is a distinctive ministry of the bishop.

While these views should be acceptable to both Lutherans and Methodists, this presentation concentrates on their Lutheran provenance. In addition, the argument also focuses on the concrete functions of ministry. Such a focus often is seen as inimical to an appreciation of episcopal succession. Part of this essay intends to show that, even from a functional perspective, episcopacy and

118

episcopal succession have a role to play in the unity and continuity of the church.

I will first look at the relation of episcopacy to the unity of the church. The relation of episcopacy to the continuity of the church will follow from its role in the church's unity. I have become convinced that questions of continuity and succession are best considered in the context of a more comprehensive discussion of ministry, episcopacy, and unity.

EPISCOPACY AND THE UNITY OF THE CHURCH

The key to the unity of the church is the gospel and its mission. The church is one as it is united in the mission of the gospel.[4] Within this unity, the pluralism of language, liturgy, custom, and theology is fully appropriate. This pluralism enriches the unity of the church when it is at the service of the church's one gospel and mission.

Essential to the mission of the gospel is the ministry of Word and Sacrament. The church needs this ministry to be church. This ministry is essential because its task is essential; it is to represent to the church the Word by which the church lives, the Word of Christ.[5] As the Augsburg Confession states:

> In order that we may obtain this faith, the ministry of teaching the Gospel and administering the sacraments was instituted. For through the Word and the sacraments, as through instruments, the Holy Spirit is given, and the Holy Spirit produces faith, where and when it pleases God, in those who hear the Gospel. (Art. 5.1–2 Latin)

This ministry must continue if the church is to exist. As BEM, sec. 8, states: "The ministry of such persons, who since very early times have been ordained, is constitutive for the life and witness of the Church."

As representative of the gospel in which the church is one, the ministry of Word and Sacrament is a ministry of unity. This ministry represents to the congregation its basis in the one gospel common to the church everywhere and at all times. As it represents the one gospel in which the church is one, the ministry is not only a sign of the unity of the church, but is also a means by which this unity is realized. As ordained ministers are one in their proclamation of the gospel in Word and Sacrament, the church is one.

The unity of the ordained ministry is thus a sign and means of the needed unity of the church.

The connection between the unity of the church and the unity of the ordained ministry points to the basis for a collegial understanding and realization of this ministry. Bernard Cooke draws this connection between ministry, unity, and collegiality well:

> Someone or some group must be in the position to witness to a given local community the faith of "the great church" today (and vice versa) and to witness to the essential continuity of faith over the centuries (i.e., to the apostolic tradition). Because they are in this "link" position, unifying the communities into "the great church," those who perform this function must do so collegially. In unique fashion they could share their faith with one another, so that each can bear witness in his [sic] own community to this communal faith and so that each can enrich this communal faith with the particular insights of his own community.[6]

No ministry is rightly carried out in a solo manner. All ministries are subject to correction and enrichment by the wider community. The ordained ministry, however, has a further collegial character. Ordained ministers are accountable one to another for how they represent that which makes the church one. As members of a synod assembly or conference, Evangelical Lutheran Church of America (ELCA) and United Methodist Church (UMC) pastors bear a direct responsibility for the mission of the church throughout the area. For all of our churches, ordination is not simply to the call or charge at hand, but to a series of such calls or charges at any place in the church. Ordination is not repeated for each new call or charge. This prospective orientation of ministry toward the entire church contributes to the collegial nature of ordained ministry. Although ordained ministry is one ministry among others, it requires that the minister have a certain independence over against any particular community. The minister must represent the Word, whether or not this Word is what the community wants to hear at the moment. Because of this needed independence, the collegial accountability of ministers one to another is all the more important. Thus, although ministry in various places is assigned to different persons, each is to carry out that ministry in a collegial unity with other ministers.

Such an understanding of the collegial nature of ordained ministry has a strong foundation in the pre-Reformation tradition and may seem obvious to Methodists. Methodist ideas and practice of itinerancy and conference connection undergird the collegiality of the ordained ministry. I have been able to find far less reflection on this idea in Lutheran sources, despite the occasional practice of organizing Lutheran synods as associations of pastors.[7] Lutheran uneasiness at any hint of the creation of a separate clerical caste may be an obstacle here.[8] Nevertheless, Lutheran practice seems to embody some aspects of a collegial understanding. Important here is the practice by which ordination to the ministry of Word and Sacrament is normally performed by ordained ministers. Entrance into the ministry requires a call from a congregation along with the approbation of other ordained ministers. Melanchthon states that it is "necessary that pastors be ordained by pastors"; ordination "without the judgment and the approbation of the pastors is in conflict both with the divine law and with the ancient church."[9] Martin Chemnitz, coauthor of the Formula of Concord, argues from both New Testament and patristic evidence that no one should enter the ordained ministry without the approval of both the people and the clergy. The call represents the approval of the people; ordination, the approval of the clergy.[10] More recently, the Roman Catholic–Lutheran Joint Commission sees in Lutheran ordination practice an implicit recognition of the collegial nature of the ordained ministry. "Since in the service of unity it [ordained ministry] stands in and between the local churches, its transmission takes place through those who are already ordained. Thus the fact that ministers can perform the service of unity only in community with other ordained ministers is expressed in this way."[11] Lutherans have then implicitly recognized the collegial character of the ordained ministry at some points in their practice. As this collegial character is realized, and the ordained ministry is one in its witness to the gospel, the oneness of the church is realized.

But what about bishops? What is the connection between the ministry of the bishop and the unity of the church in the unity of the ordained ministry? The distinctive ministry of the bishop is inevitably a ministry at the service of the unity of the church. The bishop's ministry of oversight and the bishop's ministry of unity are one ministry, one task. Since the bishop oversees the integrity of the mission of the church in a wide area, the bishop's ministry is a means and a sign of the unity of the churches in the one gospel.

The bishop's supervisory service to the unity of the church is also a collegial ministry. On the one hand, the oversight is exercised in cooperation with the other ministries within the synod or conference. Various committees and faculties play a role in this oversight. On the other hand, if the church is to be one in its mission, then the bishops need to be one in their oversight. Similar criteria need to be applied by the different bishops. If one bishop understands the mission of the church exclusively as building a just society and another understands the church's mission only as saving souls from perdition, their oversights will not contribute to the unity of their respective charges. The bishops' ministry of unity requires that they be one in their ministry. Again, their collegial responsibility one to another comes to the fore. The unity of the bishops becomes a special means and sign of the unity of the church.

The special role of the bishops in the ministry that makes the church one is crucial to the proposals of BEM, of COCU, and especially *Facing Unity*. Is intercommunion of altar and pulpit fellowship true unity in the mission of the gospel, or does unity call for "a concrete and lived-out fellowship which embraces all aspects of ecclesial life" (*Facing Unity*, sec. 89)? Intercommunion can become a mutually oblivious coexistence. Does unity in mission demand something more? The joint exercise of *episcopé* with a resultant common ordained ministry is proposed as the most ecumenically fruitful way to such a common life. If the previous analysis of the appropriate role of the bishop in the unity of the church is correct, then the unifying role ascribed to episcopacy and *episcopé* in these proposals seems justified.

EPISCOPACY AND THE CONTINUITY OF THE CHURCH

If certain complications are ignored, what has been said about episcopacy and the unity of the church can easily be transformed to apply to episcopacy and the continuity of the church. Continuity is simply unity across time. As bishops oversee the integrity and identity of the church's mission, they also oversee its continuity. For both Lutherans and Methodists the most important criterion of integrity and identity is the apostolic witness found in the New Testament. If the church's unity in this gospel is preserved, then the church's continuity is also preserved. The bishop's distinctive ministry of oversight is thus a ministry at the service of the church's continuity. When BEM describes the bishop as a minister of oversight, unity, and continuity, it is ascribing one ministry to the bishop, not three. To be a minister of oversight is to be a minister of unity and continuity.

The collegiality of ministry and its episcopal oversight, as expressed in the roles of clergy and bishop in ordination, are both means and sign of continuity. As the approbation of episcopal oversight and ministerial collegiality is expressed in ordination, each generation must approve the entry of the next into the office. A succession of ordinations is the result, a side effect of the realization of this collegiality and oversight. The unbroken continuity of ordinations is a sign of the continuity of the church in the one message. Because continuity across time is more abstract (one cannot hold a conference of first-, tenth-, and twentieth-century ministers), the symbolization of this continuity becomes particularly important. Thus, while a continuity of ordinations may be only a side effect functionally, it may be highly significant symbolically.

Unfortunately, complications that cannot be ignored disturb the picture. Continuity can take different forms. Both of the following lines exhibit a kind of continuity.

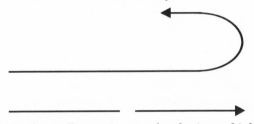

The top line is physically continuous, but by its end it has reversed the line's original direction. The bottom line is not physically continuous, but it does preserve the line's original direction. Each line exhibits a continuity the other lacks. Which continuity is more important depends on what function the line serves.

The analogy with the continuity of the church should be obvious. Most agree that a continuity like that of the second line, a continuity with the original direction or nature of the church's mission, is the decisive continuity. Episcopal or presbyteral succession of office or ordination is to serve that more fundamental continuity in the mission of the gospel. But can the two sorts of continuity come into conflict? Can the unbroken line of office or ordination drift off course so that it no longer moves in the original direction? The question is about the means God uses to preserve the church in the truth. Does God safeguard the church so that such a drift cannot occur? As Todd Nichol shows elsewhere in this text, the experience of the Reformation in continental Europe was that such a drift had occurred, especially in the case of the bishops. There the Reformation found itself forced into a choice that Catholic doctrine says cannot occur. Despite the reformers oft stated willingness and even desire to preserve continuity in episcopacy, their conclusion was that they were faced with a choice between episcopal continuity and continuity in the gospel. Since the former exists only for the sake of the latter, their decision was a foregone conclusion.

I see no way Lutherans or Methodists can reverse the judgment that a choice between continuity of episcopal office or ordination and continuity in the gospel is a possibility. Nevertheless, we should not let this issue occupy our vision so completely that other aspects of the situation are blotted out. First, implicit in the argument presented is the conclusion that collegiality of ministry and *episcopé* is a more fundamental reality and concern than succession. The decisive event in the Reformation ministerial rupture was the loss of collegiality between Catholic and Reformation ministries. The Catholic rupture occurred as decisively with episcopal England and Sweden as with non-episcopal Germany. The ecumenical goal should be the restoration of collegiality in ministry and *episcopé*. As *Facing Unity* shows, if a collegial exercise of *episcopé* is reestablished, questions of succession take care of themselves eventually (although in the meantime questions may remain problematic).

Second, the fact that any sort of succession is not a guarantee of continuity in the gospel should not blind us to the symbolic and historical reasons that warrant a recognition of the importance of some sort of succession. The unbroken succession of presbyterial ordinations that link almost all Catholic, Orthodox, and Protestant churches with the earliest church is a powerful sign that the church will always exist, that the gates of hell shall not prevail against it. Also, the church's past and present experience must carry weight. The near ubiquity in the pre-Reformation church of episcopal structures with some type of succession and their continued presence in the churches of over three-quarters of the world's Christians place the burden of proof on those who continue to find the rejection of such structures important enough to make them an obstacle to ecumenical reconciliation.[14] Warren Quanbeck summed up the attitude toward questions of succession that seems most in accord with the stated commitments of the Reformation.

> Apostolic succession in the narrower sense as succession through episcopal ordination is not a *sine qua non* of the apostolic succession of church and ministry. It does not produce an apostolic succession and authority which are missing from other types of ordination. But ordination by episcopal imposition of hands should be seen as a sign of the apostolic succession of the ministry and of the church, and therefore a sign of the unity and catholicity of the church.[15]

We should not reject the significance of the episcopal office for the church's continuity because we judge that others have exaggerated that significance.

A ROLE FOR BISHOPS IN EPISCOPACY

This paper has constituted an argument in favor of seeing bishops as appropriate focal points of the unity and continuity of the church. Assumptions have been made, most notably about the nature of ministry. If one does not view ordained ministry as representing the Word of God to the community, then this argument may not be convincing. As stated earlier, the argument as presented does not underwrite more restrictive assertions about the necessity of a certain sort of episcopacy for the unity and continuity of the church. However the view of episcopacy, unity, and continuity presented here does underwrite proposals such as BEM, *The COCU Consensus, Facing Unity,* or others of a similar type. If bishops are appropriate focal points of unity and continuity in their distinctive ministries, then church structures that utilize episcopacy as a sign and means of unity are also appropriate. Unity and continuity are important to the life of the church. We should use all the appropriate means in their pursuit.

9

Teaching Authority
in the United Methodist Church:
A Perspective

In the spring of 1986, United Methodists were startled when they read headlines announcing a pastoral letter distributed by their bishops entitled: "In Defense of Creation: The Nuclear Crisis and a Just Peace."[1] United Methodists regularly read newspaper stories about Roman Catholic bishops instructing the faithful. Rarely does the episcopal leadership in the United Methodist Church issue a pastoral letter.

Only a few pastoral letters have been circulated in the five decades since its union in 1939. No episcopal messages were forthcoming between 1942 and 1952, although United Methodist bishops continued to speak every quadrennium through the Episcopal Address to the General Conference. On the rare occasion of a pastoral letter, members understand that the content is important enough to be overheard by the world.[2]

The term magisterium is not in the regular working vocabulary of any branch of Methodism. The Council of Bishops, the collegial expression of episcopal leadership in the denomination, would never claim a teaching authority that belongs to it by reason of office. While the bishops have occasionally produced teaching documents, such as the 1986 pastoral letter, there is no equivalent to a universal authoritative teaching body in United Methodism.

Nevertheless, the care taken in the development of the 1986 pastoral letter, and the serious attention paid to the accompanying study document within the Annual Conferences, indicate that the Council of Bishops can be an effective teaching office. Are United

Methodists becoming more hospitable to their bishops exercising a stronger teaching role in the affairs of the denomination?

The remainder of this essay will explore the basis for the teaching authority of the United Methodist episcopate along three lines:

1. reviewing the historical role of the bishops in the formation of standards for faith and life in North American Methodism;
2. examining the conciliar form of teaching authority in connection with the pastoral letter of 1986;
3. suggesting areas of convergence and common teaching between Lutherans and United Methodists.

HISTORICAL ROLE OF BISHOPS

Methodism began as a reform movement within the Anglican tradition. The early identity of the sect emerged against the religious intolerance of the previous century, the agnosticism of Enlightenment philosophy, and in the context of the industrialization of eighteenth-century England. In all the "essentials of the gospel of grace," Wesley accepted and defended ideas derived from the Lutheran Reformation.[3] The young Methodist movement also adopted the strongly negative attitude of the reformers toward papal infallibility. The Methodist faith family tends to be suspicious of any ecclesiastical structure that claims immunity from error. North American Methodists began curbing episcopal power as early as in the General Conferences of 1796 and 1808.[4]

The founder of the Methodist movement, on the other hand, was notorious for the exercise of magisterial authority. On August 19, 1785, John Wesley simply declared, "I firmly believe I am a *scriptural* ἐπίσκοπος as much as any man in England or in Europe."[5] On biblical evidence (as filtered through the lenses of the scholarship of his day), and on the logical grounds of necessity (the withdrawal of Anglican clergy from the new world), John Wesley claimed the authority of *episcopé*. He wrote to Charles, "I verily believe I have as good a right to ordain as to administer the Lord's Supper."[6]

Fortified with this self-authenticating authority, John Wesley assumed the right to revise the existing doctrinal standards of the Church of England. Emissary Thomas Coke carried an abridged Sunday service and a radically altered Articles of Religion to the societies in the New World. Wesley unilaterally applied major surgery to the Articles reducing them from thirty-nine to twenty-four or twenty-five standards and substantially altering many of the survivors.

The Christian calendar was also amended by John Wesley and he changed some of the language in the Lord's Prayer. In addition, he extensively modified the baptismal liturgy, eliminated the rite of Confirmation, and removed the Catechism. John Wesley erased thirty-four psalms from the liturgical psalter and portions of fifty-eight others disappeared; these psalms were banished because Wesley decided they were "highly improper for the mouths of a Christian congregation."[7]

On March 25, 1785, John Wesley wrote, "I know myself to be as real a Christian bishop as the Archbishop of Canterbury."[8] He claimed the authority to administer sweeping powers of *episcopé*. The superintending office gave Wesley internal permission, on the grounds of his own experiential knowledge and the exigencies of a deteriorating colonial situation, to exercise the traditional teaching responsibilities of *episcopé*. Was Wesley's paring away of doctrinal standards a stunning example of religious arrogance, a reformer's hurried zeal to simplify standards for the New World, or the authoritative exercise of the teaching authority of an *episcopos*?

Whatever Wesley's motivation, the American Methodist preachers had neither the time, education, nor the inclination to challenge Wesley's revisionary pen. The Christmas Conference of 1784 adopted Wesley's excised Articles of Religion, and this version later became legally binding in the first Restrictive Rule of the General Conference of 1808.

In general, North American Methodists have not relied heavily on the Articles of Religion, which were eventually reduced from twenty-six to twenty-one articles in 1816 by the Evangelical church. A Confession of the United Brethren in Christ, brought into the union of 1946, suffers the same fate as the Articles and neither are widely studied in United Methodist congregations. For example, there are no documents in the Methodist movement to equal the authoritative force of *The Book of Concord*. United Methodists do not attach a high degree of authority to confessional writings. While regarding such documents with great respect, the church has not ascribed to the creedal statements of the ecumenical councils, to the words of our own founders, or to the confessions of other denominations as a definitive status for interpreting the gospel for our time.

Even John Wesley's Sermons and the Notes have lost their original authority and are not primary reference materials on many pastor's shelves or in church libraries. In fact, the popular piety of American Methodists has always developed in a very pragmatic way—thoroughly absorbed and grounded in the ethos of individualism, democracy, along with pluralism and accompanying ideas of relativism.

The Wesleyan standards, however they are delineated (be they the Articles and Confession alone, or the Articles, Confession, Sermons, Notes, and General Rules), are *de jure* in the denomination. United Methodists, however, operate *de facto* in a complex pattern of biblical metaphor and theological relativity. The convenient formula of the quadrilateral authorities (Scripture, tradition, reason, and experience) have functioned in this vacuum as a consensus instrument in the discussion of doctrine.

As useful as the principle of the quadrilateral has been, its application has led to individualistic interpretations in doctrinal matters. Use of the quadrilaterals does not always help a conscientious United Methodist to differentiate between what is the *plenum esse* (essential to the fullness of the church) and what is *adiaphoron* (good but not necessary), or that which John Wesley called the difference between "essentials" and "matters of opinion."[9]

These facts have left a teaching gap in North American Methodism. Until recently, many United Methodist theologians followed the scholarship of biblical scholar C. H. Dodd, who gave the impression that *kerygma* and *didache* were differentiated substantively in the ancient apostolic community.[10] Dodd asserted that apostolic preaching was accorded a higher value in the New Testament than the ethical instruction of apostolic teaching. In addition, Methodist ministers, like other Protestants, continue to be influenced by the elevation of the preached Word in neoorthodox theology. Finally, a persistent anti-intellectualism endures in the denomination, guaranteeing that teaching will continue to be accorded a lower status than preaching.

More recent scholarship has challenged Dodd's hypothesis.[11] Alarmed pastors note the state of biblical and historical illiteracy in the laity of their congregations. Many in the denomination are beginning to suspect that the recovery of Christian teaching is essential to the survival of the apostolic faith. Professional educators, such as Candler School of Theology's Professor Charles R. Foster, critique the abundance of managers and the scarcity of teachers in the denomination.[12]

It should come as no surprise that teaching has been a low priority in the Council of Bishops. The teaching ministry has also been a neglected part of the seminary education of clergy. For the most part, teaching has been assigned to the laity in local congregations. United Methodist clergy and laity alike need the witness of the Lutheran Confessions which assert that God instituted "the ministry of teaching the Gospel and administering the sacraments."[13] The Lutheran view that the teaching office (magisterium) is essentially a preaching office (*Predigtamt*) would be a helpful corrective for the disjuncture between preaching and teaching that occurs regularly in United Methodism.[14]

The educational confusion of Christians is compounded by the reality of doing ministry in the cultural diversity of the United States. The lack of purpose and direction fostered by a climate of extreme individualism in doctrinal matters has led some United Methodists to yearn for the recovery of standards from the early Wesleyan tradition. A grass roots movement urged the General Conference of 1988 to implement stronger doctrinal guidelines.

In spite of the precedent of the aggressive oversight of John Wesley, very few United Methodists looked to their bishops for educational leadership. Actually there are no effective structures for bishops to speak for the church in doctrinal decision making. Instead, a panel of theologians prepared a new doctrinal statement that was reviewed, altered, and approved by the 1988 General Conference.

United Methodist bishops, nevertheless, are not relieved from the life-long obligation as ordained elders to teach the Word under the mandate of Paragraph 439 in *The Book of Discipline*—only the sphere of their educational oversight changes and expands. A growing contingent of United Methodists believes that the Council of Bishops should seek an expanded leadership role in delineating the perplexing questions of faith and life in our times. Annual conferences would profit if their bishops took time and energy to teach regularly in pastors' schools, confirmation retreats, and laity rallies. Laity hope that bishops will exhort and press the ordained on their duty as Christian teachers. The dependable laity, steadfastly bearing much of the educational effort of the church, would welcome encouragement for their own teaching ministry from the bishop. The Council of Bishops might also prod the denomination's seminaries for a serious appraisal of how well their various curricula prepare ministers to teach. Many United Methodists also welcomed the more aggressive teaching role signaled in the pastoral letter of 1986.

CONCILIAR FORM OF TEACHING AUTHORITY

The proper teaching role of the bishops is stated vaguely in *The Book of Discipline*. The first book of discipline in 1784, for preachers in the Methodist Episcopal Church in America, stated that a general superintendent is, "to travel through as many circuits as he can, and to direct in the spiritual business of the societies." The Council of Bishops was constituted by the Conference of 1789. After the General Conference of 1816 one of the duties of the bishop, or a committee appointed by the bishop in each annual conference, was the appointment of a course of reading and study for candidates pursuing ordination.[15]

Currently, through their active role in leadership of various quadrennial programs and in the agenda of the various committees of the General Conference, the bishops function indirectly as teaching elders.[16] Through the years the administrative duties of the bishops have been methodically outlined. Exactly how much delegated power bishops have to direct the spiritual business of the denomination is no clearer now than it was in 1784.

On the other hand, the authority of the Conference is very well defined. At the very onset of the Methodist movement in America, strong historical precedents were set that gave the Conference priority over the office of bishop. Francis Asbury may not have been aware of the celebrated formula of the ancient church, "The one who would be the head of all must be chosen by all." From the time, however, Asbury insisted that the American preachers have the final voice by electing or refusing to elect a bishop to the superintending office, American Methodism turned to an ancient conciliar principle.

The present *Discipline* describes the conciliar principle as "the collective wisdom of living Christian pastors, teachers and people" which will "guard and guide the ongoing communal life." How forceful this precept has become is clear from Paragraph 610 of *The Book of Discipline* which reads: "No person, no paper, no organization, has the authority to speak officially for The United Methodist Church, this right having been reserved exclusively to the General Conference under the Constitution." Along with the familiar quadrilaterals, the conciliar principle guides United Methodists in matters of faith and practice. The General Conference, a representative gathering of the faithful, exercises a corporate teaching authority in the church.

The polity of the United Methodist Church is bound to the conciliar principle as embodied in the Conference. By church law, the instruction of the General Conference is always superior to the voice of the Council of Bishops. Irregardless, United Methodists delegate important teaching tasks to those called out of the body for the role of general superintendents. Bishops, by virtue of the office bestowed through the election of their peers, are ceded both formal and informal teaching power (although not all bishops personally understand their teaching role in the same way). This fact may be seen in the positive acceptance of the pastoral letter of 1986.

The pastoral letter "In Defense of Creation: The Nuclear Crisis and A Just Peace," was not designed to be a consensus opinion for the church or a policy statement to the denomination. The message came "from the bishops to the church as a pastoral and a prophetic word." The intent was "pastoral" in that the bishops sought to lead the church in study, prayer, and action on the issues of peace and nuclear arms. The message was "prophetic" in that it stated, through the understanding of the bishops, the Word of God to the church at this moment in history. The pastoral was not, declared the bishops, "the final word on the issue."

The assumption of the United Methodist bishops was that the authority to teach came to them not from office but from the responsibility of inner spiritual conviction. The bishops state that they undertook this task in obedience to Christ, "who is our peace." The Council used such religious expressions as: "We have been moved by the spirit of Jesus to send you a message"; and, we are "motivated by our own sense of Christian responsibility and stewardship for the world God created." These words describe an experiential way of expressing authority that fits comfortably into the position of the World Methodist Council's affirmation: "The Holy Spirit confirms the gospel in the lives of believers."[17]

During their two years of prepublication study, the bishops searched for wisdom in the Scriptures and in the historical tradition of the church. A *National Catholic Reporter's* editorial for May 9, 1986, thought that one contrast between the United Methodist and Roman Catholic approach to nuclear disarmament appeared at the point of the tradition. The writer maintained that Catholic bishops sought to square their views with the "just war" theory, pacifism and other received teachings, and papal pronouncements. "No such restrictions hampered the Methodists," said the *Reporter*, "as Methodists felt little need to reconcile their convictions with the thinking of the past."[18]

The Council did examine the three classical positions and concluded that the threefold division (pacifism, "just-war" doctrine, and crusade) were "outmoded and inadequate for clarifying the ethical dilemmas of the nuclear arms race." The bishops also appealed to their heritage as Methodists. They reviewed the position of John Wesley who believed that war was the evidence of humanity's fallen, sinful state. The Social Principles of the United Methodist Church were invoked. The framers of the pastoral letter focused some attention on the Wesleyan emphasis on personal holiness as a source for "fidelity in peacemaking." Finally, after the contemporary issues had been studied and discussed, they formulated a provisional list of guiding principles. The bishops arrived at a consensus and the vote was unanimous.

When asked by the press how much moral authority the bishops carried, Bishop C. Dale White of New York harkened to the principle that persuasion counts for more than the weight of official positions. "We command about as much moral authority as we can earn," said Bishop White.

The same premise governs the day-to-day influence of the bishops on the annual conferences in which they have oversight. The respect for a particular bishop's teaching relies heavily on personal integrity.[19] Personal credibility is a major criterion for teaching authority.

A note of caution must be added. The theological principle that the gift of teaching is rooted in the authority of baptism, and does not depend on elected office, is of particular importance to women, persons of color, and other minorities within the denomination. Until all United Methodists are able to participate equally in leadership at every level of church governance, those who have been traditionally marginalized will harbor a "hermeneutical suspicion" about teaching documents that come from noninclusive sources. These excluded groups are particularly aware of the political and conflicting perspectives that enter into decision making by well-intentioned institutional hierarchies. Those who have been left outside the system have little interest in giving more teaching power to a Council of Bishops not truly representative of the total church.

AREAS OF CONVERGENCE

The charisma of teaching belongs to the whole church. Teaching authority comes from Christ, is activated by the Holy Spirit, and resides in the community of all Christians through the Sacrament of Holy Baptism. The function of teaching belongs to the *esse* or essential being of the church. The authority to teach is exercised by all baptized believers who may delegate persons with special gifts and graces to instruct the church and world on behalf of the body.

Members of the Lutheran and Methodist movements worldwide believe that both conciliar and episcopal authority, of whatever constitution, are always subordinate to the gospel. Religious experience is rightfully judged within the Christian community by criteria drawn from Scripture and tradition. Ultimately the teaching mandate of councils and bishops comes from discerning what it means to be obedient to Christ.[20] Both churches acknowledge Scripture as the ultimate source of knowledge and authority for that call to obedience. The gospel as witnessed in the Scriptures "critically interprets experience"[21] and "is normative for all proclamation and teaching in the Church."[22]

A popular working assumption within the denomination is that the United Methodist Church derives both identity and authority from its mission. United Methodists stress the idea that the mission of the church determines the form and content of Christian teaching. Christians are called to the gospel of the justifying, sanctifying, and liberating reign of God proclaimed in the person and work of Jesus Christ. Authoritative teaching is the faithful witness to the gospel in the midst of social, cultural, and political life.

United Methodists hold that the Holy Spirit guides Christian teaching not only in the early centuries of the church's life but also in the issues that confound the contemporary church. Religious experience is an essential factor in decision making.[23] In spite of all reservations, United Methodists trust in the presence of the Holy Spirit to guide both the community and individuals in the light of the gospel.

A perception exists that Methodists have emphasized the value of religious experience under the guidance of the Holy Spirit more than Lutherans.[24] United Methodists do not apologize for holding the doctrines of justification and sanctification in creative tension. The teaching ministry of the church has been carried out in a variety of forms through the centuries. The ecclesiology of the Lutheran and Methodist branches of the church are grounded in different historical circumstances and have led to differing practices. The history of Methodism leads the denomination to a dynamic concept of authority. Dynamic authority derives its power less from institutional office or confessional statement than from participation in the mission of the church. Religious authority has power when its teaching demonstrates strength and hope in places that call for justice and righteousness.

United Methodists officially embrace diversity while encouraging unity based on the sacred *memoria* of God's gracious acts recorded in text and tradition. Both Lutherans and United Methodists face the challenge of educating for mission in a pluralistic society. In this context, both confessions attempt to bring their members an authentic understanding of the apostolic tradition contained in Scripture, the ancient creeds forged by ecumenical councils, and from the writings of commonly acknowledged fathers and mothers of the faith.

The difficulties that arise as pedagogical decisions are influenced by pluralistic authorities have led some United Methodists to a new willingness to accept a more rigorous exercise of teaching from episcopal leaders. United Methodists are fully aware that episcopal pronouncements may employ spirit-filled rhetoric while truly reflecting a sinful lack of vision. With the caution that there is likely to be a "sin instinct" as well as a "faith instinct" in such deliberations, could Lutherans and United Methodists look toward participation in a structure that would be an effective means of speaking in a more universal manner than either body has available at present?

In the future there may be a willingness on the part of United Methodists to investigate some form of ecumenical magisterium, as long as infallibility is not a hidden goal and equality of participation is assured.[25] The faith and order division of the WCC is already functioning as such a teaching institution. Lutherans and United Methodists might decide what norms could be formulated that would help both traditions in evaluating the statements of an ecumenical magisterium.

Lutherans and Methodists have much in common, especially in a shared understanding of the practice of *episcopé*. Bilateral dialogues expand the common mission interests of the two denominations and herald "preconciliar" goals. While still differing on many points, partnership in this ecumenical dialogue opens the door for common teaching.

Common teaching between Lutherans and United Methodists might center on contemporary issues of social and political justice. Both denominations share stories of a growing list of Christian martyrs. The extraordinary witness to the gospel by those who live and minister in dangerous circumstances instruct all Christians in the meaning of the cross of Christ as an identification with suffering humanity. The testimony of *martyria* calls for an identification and commitment by all Christians to oppressed people.[26]

Faith and Order of the WCC suggests that: "Churches can be strengthened by acts of teaching offered by other churches."[27] Is there a language of convergence that would allow Lutherans to accept in principle the recent pastoral letter by the United Methodist Council of Bishops as a prophetic word to the whole church? United Methodist bishops might publicly support similar efforts by the Lutheran bodies. Upholding each other's prophetic witness to church and world would be a step toward conciliar fellowship. Bearing witness together in teaching contexts visibly expresses the unity of the one catholic faith.

Notes

Chapter 1

English quotations from the Lutheran confessions are from *The Book of Concord,* ed. Theodore G. Tappert (Philadelphia: Muhlenberg, 1959). Latin quotations from the Lutheran confessions are from *Die bekenntnisschriften der evangelisch-lutherischen Kirche,* 9th ed. (Gottingen: Vandenhoeck & Ruprecht, 1982).

1. A considerably longer, more fully documented version of this paper was presented to the first session of the Lutheran–Methodist Dialogue II, meeting in Techny, Illinois on May 29—June 1, 1985. A copy of that paper may be consulted in the papers of the dialogue.
2. Augsburg Confession 5, 2–3. Hereafter referred to as CA. For a brief, but insightful introduction to the concept of the ministry in the Lutheran Confessions, see Holsten Fagerberg, *A New Look at the Lutheran Confessions (1529–1537),* tr. Gene J. Lund (Saint Louis and London: Concordia Publishing House, 1977), 226–50.
3. For Luther on the public ministry, see Wilhelm Brunotte, *Das Geistliche Amt bei Luther* (Berlin: Lutherisches Verlagshaus, 1959) and Hellmut Lieberg, *Amt und Ordination bei Luther and Melanchthon* (Göttingen: Vandenhoeck & Ruprecht, 1962). Brief surveys of the Lutheran tradition are James H. Pragman, *Traditions of Ministry; a History of the Doctrine of the Ministry in Lutheran Theology* (St. Louis: Concordia Publishing House, 1983) and John Reumann, "Ordained Minister and Layman in Lutheranism," in *Eucharist & Ministry: Lutherans and Catholics in Dialogue, IV,* ed. Paul C. Empie and T. Austin Murphy (Minneapolis: Augsburg, 1979), 227–82. For the European debate, see Holsten Fagerberg, *Bekenntnis Kirche und Amt in der deutschen konfessionellen Theologie des 19, Jahrhunderts* (Uppsala: Almquist & Wiksell, 1952). A concise summary of the American history appears in Reumann, 250–82.
4. A revealing exchange from the relatively recent history of the debate includes B. A. Gerrish, "Priesthood and Ministry in the Theology of Luther," *Church History* 34 (1965), 404–22; Lowell C. Green, "Change in Luther's Doctrine of the Ministry," *The Lutheran Quarterly* 18 (May 1966), 173–83; and Robert H. Fischer, "Another Look at Luther's Doctrine of the Ministry," *The Lutheran Quarterly* 18 (August 1966), 260–71.
5. *Luther's Works* 36, ed. Jaroslav Pelikan and Helmut T. Lehmann (St. Louis and Philadelphia: Concordia and Fortress Press, 1960–1986), 112.
6. *Luther's Works* 36, 116.
7. *Luther's Works* 44, 127, 176.
8. *Luther's Works* 44, 129.

9. *Luther's Works* 44, 128.
10. *Luther's Works* 44, 130.
11. *Luther's Works* 39, 309.
12. *Luther's Works* 40, 40.
13. *Luther's Works* 40, 41.
14. Lieberg, *Amt und Ordination*, 182.
15. *Loci Communes Theologici* in *Melanchthon and Bucer*, ed. Wilhelm Pauck, The Library of Christian Classics, Vol. 19 (Philadelphia: The Westminster Press, 1969), 61–88. In the greatly expanded version of the *Loci*, published in 1555, Melanchthon included an excursus on the public ministry. In it he declared that bishops who persecute evangelicals are not true bishops, that episcopal consecration is a wrong and erroneous custom and therefore unnecessary, that Christians ought to elect their own bishops, and that pastors need not be ordained by bishops. See *Melanchthon on Christian Doctrine: Loci Communes 1555*, ed. Clyde Manschreck, A Library of Protestant Thought (New York: Oxford University Press, 1965), 262–65.
16. *Corpus Reformatorum* 1, 763–70, ed. C. G. Bretschneider and H. E. Bindseic (Halle, 1834–1860).
17. *Corpus Reformatorum* 5, 627, trans. Paul D. L. Avis in *The Church in the Theology of the Reformers* (Atlanta: John Knox, 1981), 110. See *Corpus Reformatorum* 5, 595. Punctuation altered. On the public ministry and the place of bishops, see also Melanchthon's definitions "MINISTER EVANGELII" and "EPISCOPUS seu PASTOR" in "Definitiones Multarum Appellationum, Quarum in Ecclesia Usus Est," *Corpus Reformatorum* 21, 1087 and 1100 and *Consultation, ob die Evangelischen Fürsten einen weltlichen Frieden mit den Bischöffen annehmen, und was oder in wieferne man im Streit der Religion ihnen nachgeben könne oder nicht, Corpus Reformatorum* 3, 926–45. As had been the Wittenberg Reformation, the Consultation was signed by several theologians, including Luther.
18. *Luther's Works* 40, 313–14.
19. Lieberg, *Amt und Ordination*, 183.
20. *Luther's Works* 40, 270.
21. *Luther's Works* 40, 271.
22. CA 28, 29.
23. M. Reu, *The Augsburg Confession: A Collection of Sources with an Historical Introduction* (Chicago: Wartburg, 1930), 71–72.*
24. See his *Historical Commentary on the Augsburg Confession*, trans. H. George Anderson (Philadelphia: Fortress Press, 1986); "Die Entstehung und Erste Auswirkung von Artikel 28 der Confessio Augustana," in *Volk Gottes*, ed. Remigius Bäumer and Heimo Dolch (Freiburg: Herder, 1967); "Erwägungen und Verhandlungen über die geistliche Jurisdiktion der Bischöfe vor und während der Augsburger Reichstags von 1530," *Zeitschrift der Savigny-Stiftung für Rechtsgeschichte* 55 (1959), 348–94. A valuable discussion of Maurer's work to which I am indebted is Robert J. Goeser, "The Historic Episcopate and the Lutheran Confessions," *Lutheran Quarterly* 1 (Summer 1987), 214–32.
25. For the text of the Torgau Articles, see Henry E. Jacobs, ed., *The Book of Concord* Vol. 2 (Philadelphia: General Council Publication Board, 1883), 75–98.
26. Reu, *Augsburg Confession*, 91–97.*
27. Reu, *Augsburg Confession*, 123–126.*
28. Reu, *Augsburg Confession*, 124.*
29. Reu, *Augsburg Confession*.
30. Reu, *Augsburg Confession*, 125.*
31. Reu, *Augsburg Confession*.
32. See Theodore Kolde, *Die älteste Redaktion der Augsburger Konfession mit Melanchthons Einleitung* (Gutersloh: C. Bertelsmann, 1906). A translation of the text edited by Kolde appears in Theodore E. Schmauk and C. Theodore Benze, *The Confessional Principle and the Confessions of the Lutheran Church as Embodying the Evangelical Confession of the Christian Church* (Philadelphia: General Council Publication Board, 1911).

33. Schmauk and Benze, *The Confessional Principle*, 277.
34. Schmauk and Benze, *The Confessional Principle*, 278–9.
35. Schmauk and Benze, *The Confessional Principle*, 280–1.
36. Schmauk and Benze, *The Confessional Principle*, 282.
37. Reu, *Augsburg Confession*, 280.* Cf. also 87.
38. See notes 23 and 24 above.
39. *Corpus Reformatorum* 2, 732. In the 1541 *Variata* Melanchthon reversed himself. Georg Kretschmar has recently summarized the terms of the reversal in "The Diet of Regensburg and the 1541 Variata of the Augsburg Confession," *Piety, Politics, and Ethics: Reformation Studies in Honor of George Wolfgang Forell*, ed. Carter Lindberg (Kirksville, Missouri: The Sixteenth Century Journal Publishers, Inc. 1984), 85: ". . . Article 28 was completely reworked so that the objective was exactly the opposite from that of 1530. The article no longer determined the presuppositions and extent to which a recognition of episcopal jurisdiction in traditional medieval form is possible. Instead, in the new version it established why an episcopacy of this kind is not even needed in the new church."
40. *Luther's Works* 34, 28.
41. *Luther's Works* 34, 45.
42. *Luther's Works*.
43. *Luther's Works* 34, 51.
44. *Luther's Works*.
45. *Luther's Works*.
46. *Luther's Works* 34, 52. An illuminating analysis of Luther's attitude toward the Augsburg Confession and the proceedings at Augsburg is in Hilding Pleijel, "Luthers Inställning till *Confessio Augustana*," in *Var Kyrkas Bekännelse; Studier i Symbolik* (Lund: C. W. K. Gleerups Forlag, 1941).
47. I have relied heavily here on the analysis of Leif Grane in *The Augsburg Confession: A Commentary*, trans. John H. Rasmussen (Minneapolis: Augsburg, 1987), 156–8.
48. Apology of the Augsburg Confession 28, 13–14.
49. Apology of the Augsburg Confession 28, 7–8.
50. Apology of the Augsburg Confession 28, 3–5.
51. Apology of the Augsburg Confession 28, 20.
52. *Luther's Works* 45, 81–129.
53. CA 28, 23.
54. CA 28, 29.
55. Apology of the Augsburg Confession 7 & 8, 20.
56. Smalcald Articles III, 10, 1–2.
57. Smalcald Articles III, 10, 3.
58. Treatise on the Power and Primacy of the Pope, 62–63.
59. Treatise on the Power and Primacy of the Pope, 65–72.
60. Treatise on the Power and Primacy of the Pope, 79–82.
61. The following summary is based on the essays included in Ivar Asheim and Victor R. Gold, eds. *Episcopacy in the Lutheran Church? Studies in the Development and Definition of the Office of Church Leadership* (Philadelphia: Fortress Press, 1970).
62. See Martii Parvio, "The Post-Reformation Developments of the Episcopacy in Sweden, Finland, and the Baltic States," in Asheim and Gold, eds., *Episcopacy in the Lutheran Church?*, 239–50, note 14.
63. For a brief survey, see Sven Kjöllerström, "Bischöfe und Superintendenten in den Schwedischen Kirche," *Theologische Literatiurzeitung* 98 (May 1973) 325-32.
64. See Gordon Donaldson, " 'The Example of Denmark' in the Scottish Reformation," in *Scottish Church History* (Edinburgh: Scottish Academic Press, 1985), 60–70.
65. James L. Schaaf, in an unpublished analysis of Maurer's *Historical Commentary* prepared for LCUSA discussions of the historic episcopate.

Chapter 2

1. *The Letters of the Rev. John Wesley, A.M.*, ed. John Telford, Standard ed., 8 vols. (London: Epworth Press, 1931), 2:77, 78.
2. David C. Shipley, "The Ministry in Methodism in the Eighteenth Century," *The Ministry in the Methodist Heritage*, Board of Education of the Methodist Church, 1960, 20.
3. Colin Williams, *John Wesley's Theology Today*, (New York: Cokesbury, 1960), 146.
4. *Letters*, 7:238–9.
5. *Minutes*, 1812 Edition, I. 190.
6. The entire documentation is reproduced in Moede, *The Office of Bishop in Methodism*, (New York: Cokesbury, 1964).
7. Thomas B. Neely, *The Evolution of Episcopacy and Organic Methodism*, (1888), 105.
8. *Methodist Magazine*, 1779, 598.
9. See, for example, R. P. Heitzenrater, *The Elusive Mr. Wesley*, 2 vols. (Nashville: Abingdon Press, 1984), 2:109–110.
10. Frank Baker, *Representative Verse of Charles Wesley*, 368.
11. James K. Mathews, *Set Apart to Serve, The Role of the Episcopacy in the Wesleyan Tradition*, (Nashville: Abingdon Press, 1985), 98–108.
12. Mathews puts it this way: "He did not like the trappings of the prelate and princely bishop" . . . All this John Wesley had in mind when he wrote the "my dear Franky" letter to Asbury chiding him for adopting the title of bishop (*Letters*, 8:91), Mathews, *Set Apart to Serve*, 107.
13. Franz Hildebrandt, "The Meaning of Ordination in Methodism," *The Ministry in the Methodist Heritage*, 68, 98; quotes *Conversion of the Wesleys*, (London: 1939), 225–6.
14. John L. Nuelsen *Die Ordination im Methodismus*, (1935), 124–5.
15. Abel Stevens, *History of the Methodist Episcopal Church*, (n.d.), 197.
16. J. Robert Nelson, "Methodism and the Papacy," *A Pope for all Christians?* ed. Peter J. McCord, (New York: Paulist Press, 1976), 156.
17. *Response of the United Methodist Church to One Baptism, One Eucharist, and a Mutually Recognized Ministry*, 1977, 33.
18. Bernard Cooke, *Ministry to Word and Sacraments*, (Philadelphia: Fortress Press, 1976), 77.
19. Cooke, *Ministry*, 557.
20. John Deschner, *Structure*, an unpublished MS, IV-1, 9, 10.

Chapter 5

1. In his definitive study, *Government in the Missouri Synod* (St. Louis: Concordia, 1947), Carl S. Mundinger dispels the notion that the founders of the Missouri Synod were dependent upon the American political system. He states: "Any democratic political theories which the founders of the Missouri Synod might have entertained, they did not get from America, but from the same source from which they derived their theology and church polity, viz., from the writings of Martin Luther." (209) Again: "Though this polity was not made of contemporary German materials, much less of contemporary American materials, it was made in America, and it surely was tailor-made for the nineteenth-century American frontier." (218)

In footnote 45 on that page Mundinger cites two significant observations that bear on the above: (1) the one by H. H. Maurer in *The American Journal of Sociology*, 31 (1925), 56, who noted: "By an irony of fate, it (the Missouri Synod) rises in defense of the Jeffersonian state, the limited state, the thing that was begotten in the iniquity of rationalism." (2) the other by Carl Mauelshagen in *American Lutheranism Surrenders to the Forces of Conservatism* (Athens: University of Georgia, 1936), 204: "The Missouri Synod's congregational and synodical organization was less objectionable than that of any other to the German immigrant, who came to America prejudiced against the hierarchical and consistorial form of church administration and autocratic, political government."

Chapter 6

1. G. F. Moede, ed., *The COCU Consensus: In Quest of a Church of Christ Uniting* [COCU] (Princeton: Consultation on Church Union, 1985); *Baptism, Eucharist and Ministry* [BEM], Faith and Order Paper no. 111 (Geneva: World Council of Churches, 1982).
2. COCU 42–43; BEM Preface and 24–25.
3. The four principles appear in COCU, nn. 21–23. These principles are applied to lay and ordained persons in COCU 24–63. BEM employs the same terms, but applies them only to the ordained ministries. See BEM, nn. 26–27.
4. COCU 22a. See too, BEM 26.
5. COCU 22b. See too, BEM 26–27.
6. COCU 23. See too, BEM 26–27.
7. COCU 23 and BEM 27.
8. See the suggested parallels between polities and principles in the Commentary to BEM 26, and in the text of BEM 27.
9. *The Book of Discipline of The United Methodist Church 1988* (Nashville: The United Methodist Publishing House, 1988). The *Discipline* represents the rules which the denomination has convenanted to follow for its life together. A greater part can be changed legislatively at the quadrennial General Conferences; other portions require far more extensive procedures, as in the Constitution. The existence of episcopacy in the denomination is, incidentally, a constitutional matter, and thus unalterable under a "Restrictive Rule." How it is conceived at a particular point in history is a legislative matter for the General Conference.
10. See for example, the pamphlet, "The Historic Episcopate," produced by the Division of Theological Studies, Lutheran Council in the U.S.A., from work undertaken from 1982–1984.
11. Other expectations in their candidacy for ordination (403 and 424) and the denomination's expectations of its members (211–215) could be equally applicable to elders.
12. See, *The Ministry in the Church* issued by the Roman Catholic/Lutheran Joint Commission in 1982.
13. COCU 24, 29, 45, 52, 57.
14. See key documents in the Lutheran communion: *The Ministry in the Church* (1982), *Lutheran Understanding of the Episcopal Office* (1983), and *The Historic Episcopate* (n.d. 1985?).

Chapter 7

1. *The Letters of the Rev. John Wesley, A.M.,* ed. John Telford, 8 vols., (London: Epworth Press, 1931), 7:284.
2. Gerald F. Moede, *The Office of Bishop in Methodism,* (New York: Abingdon Press, 1964), 242–6.
3. James K. Mathews, *Set Apart to Serve,* (Nashville: Abingdon Press, 1985), 109.
4. Mathews, *Set Apart,* 85.
5. COCU, 49.
6. COCU, 49.
7. *The Book of Discipline of the United Methodist Church,* (Nashville: United Methodist Publishing House, 1984), 249.
8. Mathews, *Set Apart,* 285.
9. Mathews, *Set Apart,* 205–207.

Notes

10. Mathews, *Set Apart*, 225.
11. Mathews, *Set Apart*, 207.
12. Francis Asbury, *The Journal and Letters of Francis Asbury*, ed. Elmer T. Clark (London: Epworth Press; Nashville: Abingdon Press, 1958), 94–98. He had similar correspondence with Bishop Seabury, dated May 14, 1791, and in 1790 with Wilberforce.
13. COCU, 48, 49.
14. *Discipline*, 2404.
15. COCU, 49.
16. Joseph A. Burgess, *What is a Bishop?* Unpublished manuscript, 1984, 20.
17. Mathews, *Set Apart*, 203.
18. BEM, 26, 27.

Chapter 8

1. BEM.
2. COCU.
3. Roman Catholic–Lutheran Joint Commission, *Facing Unity: Models, Forms and Phases of Catholic–Lutheran Church Fellowship* (Geneva: Lutheran World Federation, 1985).
4. This assertion is simply a more mission-oriented version of Augsburg Confession, VII. 2.
5. Lutherans have often derived the essential character of this ministry from the assertion in Augsburg Confession, Art. V, of its divine institution. See also "Apology to the Augsburg Confession," VII. 28, 47; Warren Quanbeck, "A Contemporary View of Apostolic Succession," in *Eucharist and Ministry: Lutherans and Catholics in Dialogue, IV* (Minneapolis: Augsburg, 1979), 185; Bernhard Lohse, "Zur Ordination in der Reformation," in *Ordination und kirchliches Amt*, ed. Reinhard Mumm (Paderborn: Bonifacius–Druckerei, 1976), 13; BEM, § 11; COCU, § 54.
6. Bernard Cooke, *Ministry to Word and Sacraments: History and Theology* (Philadelphia: Fortress Press, 1976), 330.
7. For recent assertions by German Lutherans of the collegial character especially of episcopal ministry, see *Episcopacy in the Lutheran Church?*, ed. I. Asheim & V. Gold, (Philadelphia: Fortress Press, 1970), 109f.
8. A few Lutherans are willing, however, to speak of a distinct clerical *ordo* or *Stand*. See Regin Prenter, *Das Bekenntnis von Augsburg: Eine Auslegung* (Erlangen: Martin Luther Verlag, 1980), 181f; Arthur Carl Piepkorn, "The Sacred Ministry and Holy Ordination in the Symbolical Books of the Lutheran Church," in *Eucharist and Ministry*, 105.
9. *Corpus Reformatorum* 12, 490. Quoted in Piepkorn, 115, n. 24. A similar view is implied in at least the last edition of his *Loci Communes*. See *Melanchthon on Christian Doctrine: Loci Communes 1555*, trans. Clyde L. Manschreck (1965; rpt. Grand Rapids: Baker Book House, 1982), 262–5.
10. *Examination of the Council of Trent*, Part II, trans. Fred Kramer (St. Louis: Concordia Publishing House, 1978), 707–14. In their *Lutheranism: The Theological Movement and its Confessional Writings* (Philadelphia: Fortress Press, 1976), 120f, Jenson and Gritsch make the same point.
11. *The Ministry in the Church*, § 34.
12. Vatican II, *Lumen Gentium*, § 21.
13. Vatican II, *Lumen Gentium*, § 28.
14. I would argue on theological and general philosophical grounds that while the consensus or near-consensus of past and present experience is never infallible, the burden of proof rests on those who call that consensus into question. Burdens of proof can be met, of course. That is precisely how knowledge progresses.

15. *Eucharist and Ministry: Lutherans and Catholics in Dialogue, IV* (Minneapolis: Augsburg, 1979), 187. In the limited sense noted above, one should also add "means" to "sign."

Chapter 9

1. Three documents including a pastoral letter, a foundation document and a guide for study and action were released by Abingdon Press on July 1, 1986.
2. Most of the episcopal messages have been one to three page letters without foundational documents. The topics have been wide-ranging, based on the current national or international situation, including: a war-time message to the church in December 1941; against McCarthyism on December 11, 1953; in support of the declaration of the Supreme Court abolishing segregation in the public school on November 20, 1954; and a message on November 12, 1974, reminding the denomination that evangelism is every Christian's responsibility. The messages are compiled by the Office of the Secretary of the Council of Bishops of the United Methodist Church but are unpublished.
3. Gordon Rupp, "Confessio Augustana—A Methodist Appraisal," in *The Augsburg Confession in Ecumenical Perspective* LWF Report 6/7, 1980, 92. Also see: K. James Stein, "Martin Luther and the Beginnings of United Methodism," *Explor*, Spring, 1986, 31–39.
4. Gerald F. Moede, *The Office of Bishop in Methodism, Its History and Development* (Zurich: Publishing House of the Methodist Church, 1964), 70–83.
5. *The Letters of the Rev. John Wesley, A.M.*, ed. John Telford, Standard ed., 8 vols. (London: Epworth Press, 1931), 7:284.
6. Wesley, *Letters.*
7. *John Wesley's Sunday Service of the Methodists in North America*, The Methodist Bicentennial Commemorative Reprint of *Quarterly Review* with an introduction by James F. White (Nashville: The United Methodist Publishing House, 1984), 18.
8. Wesley, *Letters*, 7:262.
9. Early English Methodism set the tone for the future in its adoption of the tolerant temper of the age in contrast to the bigotry of the seventeenth century. Gordon Rupp writes, "As a church, therefore, Methodism has not done much in the way of heresy hunting, and has always firmly decided to live and let live in what John Wesley called matters of 'opinion'—which do not, however, include the essentials of faith." Gordon Rupp, "Confessio Augustana—A Methodist Appraisal," 86.
10. C. H. Dodd, *The Apostolic Preaching and its Developments* (London: Hodder & Stoughton, 1936); Gospel and Law: the Relation of Faith and Ethics in Early Christianity (New York: Columbia University Press, 1951).
11. John Reumann, "Teaching Office in the New Testament? A Response to Professor Fitzmeyer's Essay," in Paul C. Empie, T. Austin Murphy, and Joseph A. Burgess eds., *Teaching Authority and Infallibility in the Church: Lutherans and Catholics in Dialogue VI* (Minneapolis: Augsburg, 1978, 1980), chapter 11.
12. Charles R. Foster, "Abundance of Managers—Scarcity of Teachers" *Religious Education* vol. 80, no. 3, Summer, 1985.
13. Eric W. Gritsch, "Lutheran Teaching Authority: Past and Present," *Teaching Authority and Infallibility in the Church*, 140.
14. Gritsch, *Lutheran Teaching Authority.*
15. *Journal: General Conference of 1916*, 1:151; Also see James K. Mathews, *Set Apart to Serve, The Role of the Episcopacy in the Wesleyan Tradition* (Nashville: Abingdon Press, 1985), 249–53.
16. For a clarification of episcopal organization consult Roy H. Short, *The Episcopal Leadership in United Methodism* (Nashville: Abingdon Press, 1985) and Roy H.

Short, *History of the Council of Bishops of The United Methodist Church, 1939–1979* (Nashville: Abingdon Press, 1980).

17. *The Church: Community of Grace, Lutheran–Methodist Dialogue, 1979–1984* (Geneva: Lutheran World Federation and Lake Junaluska, N.C.: World Methodist Council, 1984), 11.

18. *The National Catholic Reporter,* May 9, 1986, vol. 22, no. 28, 1.

19. United Methodists would concur with sentiments of *The Venice Statement, An Agreed Statement on Authority in the Church, an Anglican–Roman Catholic Document* (Washington D.C.: The United States Catholic Conference, 1977). The premier teaching authority of a bishop should be designated to persons with personal credibility, that is, to those who exhibit the power of personal holiness, who demonstrate the gifts of the Spirit, and who are charged to do so by ordination (including *episcopé,* "oversight").

20. Might the renewed emphasis on individual discernment by Catholic moral theologians be a helpful addition to the more evangelical language of the eighteenth and nineteenth centuries. I am thinking especially of Karl Rahner's "the faith instinct" found in *Theological Investigations,* vol. IX.

21. *The Church: Community of Grace,* 11.

22. *Teaching Authority and Infallibility in the Church,* Convergence 2, 31.

23. John Wesley wrote in his *Journal,* May 11, 1739: "The Spirit of God not only once inspired those who wrote, but continually inspires, supernaturally assists, those that read it with earnest prayer."

24. From the first, Methodists have been subject to charges of subjectivism and have always countered with a staunch defense of the "gospel of grace." The charge that Methodists were teaching "justification by feeling," was particularly strong in the early nineteenth century. Thomas A. Langford, *Practical Divinity, Theology in the Wesleyan Tradition* (Nashville: Abingdon, 1983), chapter 8.

25. Will recovery of Wesleyan doctrinal standards substantially change the direction of the denomination? My hunch is that recovery will be important only in a limited way. Popular piety in United Methodism will continue on its pragmatic way, thoroughly absorbed and grounded in the ethos of pluralism. I am not convinced that this de facto situation is to be mourned. The ministry no longer moves within the framework of Patristic, Reformation or eighteenth-century thought. Ecumenical ferment caused by Faith and Order Paper no. 111, *Baptism, Eucharist and Ministry* is more important to United Methodist liturgical life than the abridged Sunday Service of John Wesley. New-Old standards may in fact feed only those who look to nineteenth-century fundamentalist revivalism as their theological home and who yearn to locate "heretics." Beyond that is the problem of demythologizing scripture and tradition, for as Gordon Rupp so well states, "the question facing us all is that of the restatement of our anthropology in terms which no longer posit a historical basis to the myth of Adam—the kind of problem which Edmund Schlink has to deal with in the footnotes in his great work on the Lutheran confessions as theological documents." (Rupp, "Confessio Augustana," 93).

26. Suggestions for Acts of Common Teaching may be found in, "How Does the Church Teach Authoritatively Today?" Faith and Order Paper No. 91 printed in *The Ecumenical Review,* vol. 31, January 1979, 91.

27. "How Does the Church Teach?" 90.